What to Do When People Become Difficult

Even if the Difficult Person is You

And much more....

Kenneth R. Petrucci, MSW

Why is this book a unique approach to dealing with people when they become difficult?

First, this book is a **guide** that systematically outlines **immediate, useful** and **practical** approaches to dealing with people when they become difficult.

Second, this book encourages us to also **accept responsibility** for any part of the difficult situation that we created.

Third, this book helps us to study many interrelated topics that help to build a strong inner self. Some of the topics covered are these: discovering your inner strengths and weaknesses, gaining insights into human behavior, why people become difficult, how difficult behavior can hurt us, 220 phrases to use when responding to a person who is being difficult, assertiveness skills, indirect and direct communication, confrontation vs. cooperation, listening skills, a self-help process that can help people discover the root causes of many of their problems including weight gain, gambling, smoking, alcohol, substance abuse, compulsive shopping, controlling anger, problem solving, and features the Inner Peace Relaxation Technique. This book also includes many of Kenneth Petrucci's quotations which help the reader to gain insights into life and to live more effectively and successfully.

*"Some people
enter our lives like
angels with answers
to our prayers."*

Kenneth R. Petrucci, MSW

Subjects Covered

While reading this book, <u>please check off or highlight what is significantly important to you.</u> In the last chapter of this book, you will enter the "Independent Self-Study and Self-Discovery" section. Please insert the checked off or highlighted sentences in the chapter "Independent Self-Study and Self-Discovery." You may choose to highlight any statements in the book that appeal to you, including the quotations. **Remember,** if you checked off anything in this book you did so because you may need to work or reflect upon the wisdom of the writings.

<u>**Page**</u>

When studying new principles, it is best to simply apply them and let the principles prove or disprove themselves.

A FORMULA FOR SUCCESS:

BE CORRECT

BE PATIENT

BE PERSISTENT

LEARN FROM THE PAST,

PLAN FOR THE FUTURE,

LIVE IN THE PRESENT.

A NEW BEGINNING

Let no one define you before you define yourself.

Some extreme problems require extreme remedies.

Let's put the past behind us and have a new beginning.

What lesson do I need to learn from this mistake so I will not repeat it?

Let's smile to generate our own happiness.

Never pass up the opportunity to laugh.

FORGIVENESS ALLOWS US TO LET GO

The lack of forgiveness can create negative thinking which can be harmful to our physical and emotional wellbeing.

The person I need to forgive, and why --

_____
_____
_____

Resentment(s) I need to forgive --

_____
_____
_____

Grudges I need to forgive –

_____
_____
_____

The anger I need to let go of --

_____
_____
_____

I forgive myself for --

_____
_____
_____

Signature:_____**Date:**_____

**Remember,
Sometimes we forget to forgive ourselves.
Forgiveness is a gift we give to ourselves.
<u>Let's forgive ourselves and others, and
let the healing begin.</u>**

If we are considering not forgiving someone, we can ask ourselves this one question ... Do we know anyone who is perfect?

Smart forgiveness is remembering why we needed to forgive.

IF YOU WANT SOMETHING IN LIFE... TRY ASKING FOR IT. WHAT WOULD YOU LIKE TO ASK FOR?

Make a list and go for it ...

1. _____

   _____

2. _____

   _____

3. _____

   _____

PROFILE OF
KENNETH R. PETRUCCI, MSW

Kenneth R. Petrucci, MSW, is a psychotherapist with a **unique background and distinguished credentials.** He earned an Associate's Degree A.A. in Liberal Arts from the Community College of Rhode Island; a Bachelor of Fine Arts Degree B.F.A, with a major in Oral Interpretation from the Speech and Drama Department at the University of Memphis, and a Master's Degree MSW in Clinical Social Work from the University of Houston.

As a gifted young writer, Ken was considered a child prodigy as evidenced by the _Houston Chronicle_ on January 24, 1978 _by Betty Ewing_—"Petrucci ... wrote a poem at age 16 that was accepted by the prestigious _Chicago Tribune_ *poetry corner" on June 2, 1974 by Marcia Lee Masters, Poetry Editor.*

This poem, "Richest and Poorest," appears in his first book Soul's Eye, which includes innovative illustrations by Glenn Pacitto. The original printing of Soul's Eye is in a library Special Collection status because of its high quality and rarity, making it difficult to replace, thus valuable. Soul's Eye is being preserved and can be found in the following libraries: John Hay Library at Brown University, Providence, Rhode Island; McWherter Library at the University of Memphis, Memphis, Tennessee; Hillman Library at the University of Pittsburgh, Pittsburgh, PA; and located within the Glenn Coffield Papers Collection at the Knight Library, University of Oregon in Eugene, Oregon.

Ken has been asked to run for political office, and is periodically stopped by people who indicate to him that he resembles the popular actor Joe Pesci.

Ken performed stand-up comedy in his twenties. He has a track record of being an entertaining and provocative guest on radio and TV talk shows, and hosted *The Creative Connection*, a self-development talk show for four years on KPFT 90.1 FM in Houston, Texas. This radio broadcast was one of the longest running self-development radio talk shows in the United States. Ken's guests included leaders in human potential and self-improvement, along with stars such as Ray Charles, Carol Channing, Mickey Rooney, Joan Rivers, and JoAnne Worley. Mr. Petrucci's legendary interview with Ray Charles is registered in the United States Copyright Office in the Library of Congress.

Mr. Petrucci designed and taught classes at the Rhode Island Municipal Police Academy involving psychological principles to new recruits. He was a psychotherapist for more than ten years in the Providence School System in Rhode Island which had a culturally and age diversified population.

Ken wrote a newspaper column that allowed people to ask questions about how to handle stressful times in their lives. He was an award-winning salesman in educational sales, and is the founder of the Kenneth Petrucci Seminars, which were presented for twenty years at corporations, organizations, and colleges such as Brown University, the University of Houston, and the Rhode Island Dental Association.

The Kenneth Petrucci Seminars presented over ten consecutive years at the Community College of Rhode Island were one of the longest seminar series presented at a college in the United States.

In order to advance his education, Ken struggled to acquire the financial capability to attend college and worked various jobs to afford all expenses for his three degrees. If you are in school, perhaps Ken's financing of his degrees may be an encouragement to you. Furthering your education may be difficult for you but developing a plan and creating manageable goals may help you to succeed. This book will be a great asset to you because it will give you the necessary skills to be effective in life.

A NEW WORLD

IN THIS WORLD, IF WE CAN LEARN TO RESPECT
THE DIFFERENCES OF OPINIONS EACH OF US
HAS, WE CAN BECOME A MORE TOLERANT
AND HARMONIOUS SOCIETY.

(2015)

World vision of Kenneth R. Petrucci, MSW

My Cherished Reader:
Is your brain being very
intellectual today?
Here is some space for your
thoughts.

Remember,
We sometimes can avoid a confrontation by changing the topic of a conversation.

When courtesy makes a difference.........

REMEMBER, SAYING "PLEASE" AND "THANK YOU" ALONG WITH GOOD MANNERS CAN BE EFFECTIVE WITH PEOPLE WHO APPRECIATE THE RESPECT.

I am the proud owner of this life-changing, self-realization, self-improvement, self-study and self-development book.

_____

Owner's name

A LESSON FROM THE LATE MUSIC GENIUS, RAY CHARLES ON

HOW TO PUT OUR INSECURITIES ASIDE AND ACHIEVE

OUR DREAMS.....

"Ray Charles, your life was an example of true courage. Without your eyesight you made your dreams come true and became a legend. You and your music will forever be in our hearts. "

Comment by Kenneth R. Petrucci, MSW, psychotherapist and radio talk show host, after interviewing the legendary Ray Charles.

Disclaimer

The purpose of this book is to educate an individual in dealing with difficult behavior. This publication is not a substitute for mental health counseling. The publisher and author are not providing any professional services of any kind nor any guarantees by the use of this book. Therefore, no diagnosis or treatment is presented in this publication. All readers should consult their own practitioners before utilizing any of the content in the following chapters. The reader releases the publisher and author of any and all liability, including, but not limited to loss, injury or damage by the reading or use of this book.

ISBN: 069221187X

ISBN 13: 9780692211878

Library of Congress Catalog Card Number: 2014956213

Wisdom Wagon, Warwick RI

Published in the United States of America

Published by

Wisdom Wagon

www.wisdom-wagon.com

We Deliver Wisdom Worldwide

email: info@kennethpetrucci.com

BUT I WANT TO BE A
BETTER LISTENER....

POOR LISTENING CAN
BE THE RESULT OF NOT
BEING ABLE TO RELAX.

IF YOU HAVE AN ISSUE
WITH RELAXATION
PLEASE REFER TO
THE INNER PEACE
RELAXATION TECHNIQUE
IN THIS BOOK.

A TRUE FRIEND...

A true friend will tell you what you <u>need</u> to hear, not what you <u>want</u> to hear.

LET'S AGREE TO...

If someone is not following your plan you need to seek an agreement so your plan will be followed.

> *"A quote may enter our lives because we need to live it."*
>
> **Kenneth R. Petrucci, MSW**

**Awareness is so important...
Let's strive to become
more aware because
problem-solving begins with awareness.**

Saying NOTHING

may sometimes

be the best solution

to a problem.

Doing NOTHING

may sometimes

be the best solution

to a problem

In general we always want to take steps to solve our problems. However, it's important to recognize when some problems are currently too fragile and unmanageable and immediate interventions could make matters worse.

> *"Each day is an opportunity for a new beginning."*
>
> **Kenneth R. Petrucci, MSW**

> *"Sometimes it's not how little we have, but what we do with what we have."*
> **Kenneth R. Petrucci, MSW**

I am overwhelmed ...<u>now</u> what do I do?

Motivation and Momentum can be achieved by accomplishing one small goal at a time. Therefore, focus on one small achievement at a time, not on the overall goal which can be overwhelming. Like a snowball rolling downhill, one small desired goal achieved creates momentum toward your final purpose.

> *"Sometimes the distance between failure and success is two inches of patience."*
>
> **Kenneth R. Petrucci, MSW**

EFFECTIVE CONFRONTATION IS

STAYING FOCUSED ON THE FACTS

WITHOUT BEING CRITICAL

My Cherished Reader:
Space for your precious
thoughts ...

Benefits of Being Able to Deal with Difficult Behaviors

- ❖ Promotes better **health** in **general**.
- ❖ Helps us to be more in **control** of our lives.
- ❖ Increases the possibility of improving our **self-esteem**.
- ❖ Allows us to gain **self-respect**.
- ❖ Increases the possibility of **succeeding** in our chosen **career**.
- ❖ Enables us to **teach** others about how to handle difficult behavior.
- ❖ Provides another skill to use when **solving problems**.
- ❖ Helps us to improve our **relationships** with others.
- ❖ Enables us to be more **effective** in achieving our goals.
- ❖ Helps us to deal with **addictive behaviors** such as weight gain, because it enables us to gain more control of our lives and focus on handling our compulsions.
- ❖ Helps us to learn the verbal skills to be assertive enough to avoid being **abused**.
- ❖ Helps children to deal with **bullies** at school or helps adults who feel **intimidated** by other people.
- ❖ Enables us to have more mental **energy** because we are not being emotionally or mentally drained by dealing with difficult behavior.
- ❖ Enables us to **think** more clearly because we will not be preoccupied with the negativity of difficult behavior.

- ❖ Enables us to handle **stress** better.
- ❖ Improves our **image** because we are now able to be more confident in our dealings with others.
- ❖ Improves our ability to be **financially** secure because being able to handle adversity may allow us to select a better career, or to be eligible for advancement within an organization or business.
- ❖ Improves our ability to be **organized** because we are not struggling with difficult behavior.

*"Let's do a little less judgin',
and a lot more lovin'."*

Kenneth R. Petrucci, MSW

*"For someone to expect perfection
from an imperfect world is unrealistic
and creates misery."*

Kenneth R. Petrucci, MSW

Self-Assessment Questionnaire: Identifying Your Inner Strengths and Weaknesses

* Please be <u>honest</u> with yourself in answering these questions.

* Circle the number that reveals your true self.

1. Do you often seek the **approval** of other people?

    Seldom 1 2 3 4 5 6 7 8 9 10 Always

*People who choose higher numbers may be overly seeking the approval of others. It's normal to want to be liked, but the problem is that in doing so your **self-esteem** may be lost in the process.*

2. Do you typically decide not to follow your **decisions** because someone else believes that your decisions are incorrect?

    Seldom 1 2 3 4 5 6 7 8 9 10 Always

People who choose higher numbers may be more interested in other people's opinions rather than trusting their own judgment. It's good to gather the **opinions** of people qualified to judge your problem. However, in the end, your opinion is also valuable.

3. Do you let other people **limit** your goals in life?

    Seldom 1 2 3 4 5 6 7 8 9 10 Always

People who choose higher numbers may be letting other people limit their full potential.

4. Do you accept **responsibility** for your actions?

    Seldom 1 2 3 4 5 6 7 8 9 10 Always

People who choose lower numbers may be failing to accept responsibility for their actions. The moment we accept responsibility for our actions is the moment we gain control of achieving our goals.

> *"If we take one step forward, it is better than no steps at all."*
>
> **Kenneth R. Petrucci, MSW**

5. Are you willing to take some **risks** to achieve your goals?

Seldom 1 2 3 4 5 6 7 8 9 10 Always

People who choose lower numbers may be insecure about taking risks. It's important to assess whether we are willing to accept the benefits or backlash of risk-taking. The reality is that some goals require us to take risks in order to achieve them.

6. Do you have a tendency to **prejudge** solutions rather than acting on a solution?

Seldom 1 2 3 4 5 6 7 8 9 10 Always

People who choose higher numbers may be prejudging their solutions before they have a chance to have the solutions prove themselves.

7. Do you allow yourself the opportunity to be **creative** in solving difficult problems?

Seldom 1 2 3 4 5 6 7 8 9 10 Always

People who choose lower numbers may need to improve their creative approaches to life's difficult problems.

8. When you are dealing with the difficult behavior of someone, can you place yourself in his or her **position?**

Seldom 1 2 3 4 5 6 7 8 9 10 Always

People who choose lower numbers may find it difficult to listen to a problem from another person's point of view.

9. Do you find it difficult to say what you truly **feel** and **think?**

Seldom 1 2 3 4 5 6 7 8 9 10 Always

People who choose higher numbers might find it difficult to express their true thoughts and feelings.

10. Are you willing to take **small** steps if necessary to solve a problem?

Seldom 1 2 3 4 5 6 7 8 9 10 Always

People who choose lower numbers may find it difficult to begin solving a problem.

An obstacle can be an opportunity for growth.

> *"Sometimes to be successful we need to be flexible."*
>
> **Kenneth R. Petrucci, MSW**

BEFORE LOSING AN OPPORTUNITY...
Like eating a bowl of hot soup, seize an opportunity before it cools off.

Do you have opportunities cooling off? If so, list them.

1.

2.

3.

4.

5.

WHY PEOPLE BECOME DIFFICULT

- We may have **physical, psychological,** or **emotional** issues.
- We may have **limitations** or **disabilities** that can cause us to appear more difficult.
- We may be **unsure** of how to handle a certain situation.
- Others' opinions may **influence** us, which in turn can cause us to become difficult.
- We may simply lack the **knowledge** to deal with problematic issues.
- We may be **duplicating** our parents' difficult behavior patterns.
- We may simply **choose** to become difficult.
- We may be **repressing** inner subconscious issues that have never been resolved.
- When someone does or says something that threatens our values or beliefs, we can take a strong oppositional position. We may appear difficult when it is only a question of our **values** or **beliefs**.
- A younger person can appear difficult when trying to find his or her **identity**.
- A youth can also appear difficult when trying to **mimic** troubled friends.
- We may be feeling **insecure** or lacking **confidence**.

- We may feel **frightened**.
- We may be **physically** tired, consumed with **stress**, or overwhelmed with **worries**. All of these factors can cause us to become difficult.

The first step in making changes is being willing to change.

> *"The bridge we burn today may be the bridge we need to walk over tomorrow."*
>
> **Kenneth R. Petrucci, MSW**

A SYSTEM FOR SUCCESS

1. Remain firm in what you believe you can accomplish.

2. Create manageable goals.

3. Establish relationships with people with some of your common goals, allowing you both to benefit and grow together.

4. Stop overly evaluating and start taking action.

5. Continuously learn about your area of pursuit.

6. Be willing to sacrifice to achieve your goals to reap the rewards.

7. Never let anyone steal or destroy your dreams.

8. Success achieved!

How Continuous Difficult Behavior Can Hurt Us

I define excessive difficult behavior as behavior that is consistently overwhelming as opposed to dealing with daily encounters with difficult behavior.

- Dealing with continuous difficult behavior may weaken our **immune systems.**
- Continuous difficult behavior can create tension in our relationships with people. We can be **uptight** with people when our nerves are shaken by excessive difficult behavior.
- Continuous difficult behavior can cloud our ability to make **choices.** Our mind is struggling to stay mentally sound when excessive difficult behavior is draining it.
- Continuous difficult behavior can promote weight gain or stimulate **addictive** behavior in general.
- Continuous difficult behavior may cause problems in **managing** our own mental health issues.
- Continuous difficult behavior may potentially **age** us before our time.
- Continuous difficult behavior may lead to acts of **violence**.
- Continuous difficult behavior can lead to **dysfunctional** families.

- Continuous difficult behavior may cause **physical illness**.
- Continuous difficult behavior may lead to **relationship** problems in general.
- Continuous difficult behavior may promote the possibility of performing poorly at **school**.
- Continuous difficult behavior may **limit** our ability to achieve our goals.

"How we treat ourselves is sometimes how people treat us."
Kenneth R. Petrucci, MSW

"Sometimes we choose to believe a lie rather than to accept the truth."
Kenneth R. Petrucci, MSW

Insights into Human Nature

- It may be difficult to work with some people at any given time. They may be completely stubborn or unfortunately have **limitations**, such as mental health issues. We may need to acknowledge that the situation is too **difficult** to resolve at this time.
- Respecting the status of people is okay. However, if we place ourselves in a lower **self-esteem** position, we may make decisions that are incorrect for our success or safety.
- The real factors that motivate people are sometimes not **revealed** or **understood**.
- Sometimes it's best to sit down with people who are upset and ask them if they know what's **bothering** them.
- Some people don't **know** why they are being difficult.
- Our self-esteem may be **low**, making it difficult to express our needs and desires.
- Asking someone to **suggest a solution** enables them to feel they have arrived at his or her own conclusion.
- If we don't **forgive** someone, we may be giving that person some control of our lives.

- Smile when someone is attempting to upset you. This **disarms** people who need the satisfaction of angering you.
- When we put someone above us, we are automatically **below** him or her.

> *"Sometimes we can change a reality by how we perceive it."*
>
> **Kenneth R. Petrucci, MSW**

- Listen to the **whole person** when people are speaking. Their emotions, body language, and eyes are speaking simultaneously. Remember, we can't hide our eyes. As the saying goes, "The eyes are the windows to the soul."
- If we are not getting anywhere in solving a problem, it seems that we should **change** our approach. In order to make a change, we need to make changes.
- Some people may need to feel in control of themselves at all times. We may need to feed their **egos** before concentrating on the issues.
- Look for a **pattern** in people's behavior. We may recognize that difficult behavior has a pattern to it.
- Some people will hear only what they **want** to hear.
- Sometimes it's best to develop a plan of how you will deal with a person who is being difficult rather than try to **change** that person.

- Our **labels** or **beliefs** about life's situations may be keeping us from viewing our problems from a different point of view.
- Remember, we don't always know why people are upset, and they may be **uncertain** why they are upset. There are many motivations and triggers in a person's psyche.

> *"At birth the clock is set. How we choose to use our time can determine our successes or failures."*
>
> **Kenneth R. Petrucci, MSW**

> *"We need to communicate more of our thoughts and feelings rather than expecting people to automatically know what we are thinking and feeling in our hearts."*
>
> **Kenneth R. Petrucci, MSW**

- We should try to identify the **real** issues, which may not be so apparent. For example, a wife may be upset with her husband about his lack of communication with her, but the real reasons for his anxiety may be about the money matters in their marriage. The real reasons may even be rooted in their unfinished, unresolved traumas or issues of the past.

- People are like onions; they have many **layers**.
- What a person appears to be and what they truly are may be very **different**.
- If we want to know why a person is acting in a certain way, the most accurate approach is to ask the person **directly**.
- Some people comprehend better by **hearing**, others by **seeing**, and still others by being **physically** involved in trying to learn.
- Sometimes we need to explain the **reasons** for our request. This may appeal to a person's need for a logical explanation.
- It is easier to **assume** rather than to take the time *to understand*; therefore, what we hear from people may be based on assumptions, not facts.
- Some people try to make us **lose** our tempers so we will be out of control and they can win an argument.

> *"If we are in this world to help each other, then why can't we just ask for what we want?"*
>
> **Kenneth R. Petrucci, MSW**

- If we know someone is going to be difficult, we should try to select an **environment** that won't give this person an edge over us. An example is when an individual is very comfortable in his or her own environment; he or she may feel more powerful, perhaps causing us to be less confident.
- If someone continues to abuse us, the question is **why** are we allowing ourselves to be abused?
- Remember, a person's **past** behavior may be an indication of his or her future behavior.
- Some people may not want us to succeed because subconsciously they are **jealous** of us. They will perhaps make an attempt to limit us.
- We sometimes need **more information** to solve a problem.
- Sometimes we are not accepting responsibility for our actions. We need to accept responsibility for our **part** in solving a problem.
- Some people respond without thinking. They **automatically** respond to life's situations without taking time to think things through.
- Sometimes it's better to just let people **be** who they are.

- I interviewed couples who were married for many years. The one common denominator in their marriage that they attributed to their success was simply to **give and take**.

> *"Sometimes our environment is shaping us in ways of which we are unaware."*
>
> **Kenneth R. Petrucci, MSW**

Self-Assessment: Take Responsibility for Your Actions

1. Can you admit you have a problem?

    Seldom 1 2 3 4 5 6 7 8 9 10 Always

If you can't admit that you have a problem, it becomes difficult to begin a plan that will lead to a resolution.

2. Does your ego stand in the way of dealing with life's difficulties?

    Seldom 1 2 3 4 5 6 7 8 9 10 Always

Sometimes our inflated egos keep us from admitting that we could have a problem.

3. Do you complain over and over again without seeking a resolution?

    Seldom 1 2 3 4 5 6 7 8 9 10 Always

It may be easier for you to complain about a problem than to attempt to solve it.

4. Do you occupy yourself with other activities to avoid dealing with a problem?

    Seldom 1 2 3 4 5 6 7 8 9 10 Always

We sometimes keep ourselves busy to justify not having the time to deal with a problem.

5. Are you willing to accept the work or sacrifice it takes to achieve your goals?

    Seldom 1 2 3 4 5 6 7 8 9 10 Always

Sometimes we do not accept the work or sacrifice required to achieve our goals.

> "Sometimes we need to experience a tragedy to learn the meaning of gratitude."
>
> **Kenneth R. Petrucci, MSW**

Preparing to Approach a Person Who Is Becoming Difficult

The difficult situation is as follows::

_____

_____

_____

_____

_____

_____

_____

Clarify the specific issues.

_____

_____

_____

_____

_____

_____

_____

Gather information and facts regarding the situation.

_____

_____

_____

_____

_____

_____

_____

Prioritize what is most important to you.

_____

_____

_____

_____

_____

_____

Establish a timeline for various steps and eventual completion.

_____

_____

_____

_____

_____

_____

We can use the phrases or strategies from the upcoming chapter entitled "220 Persuasive Phrases to Use When People Become Difficult."

_____

_____

_____

_____

_____

_____

_____

_____

"A caring heart sometimes needs a rational mind to protect it."

Kenneth R. Petrucci, MSW

AN INSTRUCTIONAL GUIDE TO PERSUASIVE COMMUNICATION

Remember these nine points when working with the prepared phrases:

1. **Pause** after your delivery, allowing the person to digest your comments.
2. Don't **speak** too fast. This will make it difficult for a person to understand and process your statements.
3. If necessary, **repeat** your comments if the person is not understanding you.
4. Try to create an **environment** that makes it easier to communicate.
5. When speaking, remember that your **tone** of voice, volume, and body language will determine how you are interpreted.
6. Use **humor** when appropriate to the person or situation to release tension. It is difficult to be confrontational with someone who is making you laugh.
7. Whenever possible, try to **prepare** your approach when dealing with people who may become difficult.
8. The phrases you select for delivery will **depend** on the situation, personalities, and environment you are in.

9. **Practice** all the phrases, and the type of phrase to use will become apparent. You can also develop your own response to a person who is being difficult, which may be easier after learning the psychology presented in this book.

10. In general, having the opportunity to observe someone's **personality** or body language may be helpful in relating to that person. If someone appears intense you may wish to make your points without hesitation. If an individual seems to be more laid back you may be able to move at a slower pace.

> *"Remember, it is what you say and how you say it."*
> **Kenneth R. Petrucci, MSW**

> *"Each day is an opportunity to appreciate what we have."*
> **Kenneth R. Petrucci, MSW**

220 *PERSUASIVE* *Phrases to Use When people become difficult*

REPEAT PHRASES AS NEEDED.

BEFORE DISCUSSING THE ISSUE(S) BE CERTAIN THAT YOUR FACTS ARE CORRECT.

REMEMBER TO PAUSE AFTER REPEATING THESE PHRASES TO ALLOW A PERSON TO THINK ABOUT WHAT YOU SAID.

1. What can I do to regain your trust?
(Effective when you want to regain someone's respect.)

2. We need to correct some problems first before we can move forward.
(Effective when you want to establish priorities.)

3. My solution is...
(Effective when you want to confront an issue.)

4. Thank you for informing me about these problems.
(Effective when you want to show appreciation for someone's help.)

5. Your comments make a lot of sense.
(Effective when you want to comment on the common-sense approach to solving the problem.)

6. I agree with you.
(Effective when you want to get to the point.)

What is life trying to teach us?

7. From that standpoint, I understand...
(Effective when you want to express your point of view without taking a position.)

8. Can we please develop an alliance between us?
(Effective when you want to develop a partnership to solving problems.)

9. Can we roll up our sleeves and tackle these problems?
(Effective when you want to take a quick-action approach.)

10. May I ask another question?
(Effective when you want to give the other person some control in solving problems.)

27

11. May I make a suggestion?
(Effective when you want to give the other person some control in solving problems.)

12. It's time to let out some steam. I'll call you in three days. (State the timeframe.)
(Effective when you want to create some space to allow a person the opportunity to unwind.)

We are all intelligent,
but in different ways.

13. I respect your level of intelligence. How would you handle this?
(Effective when you want someone to feel he or she can be a partner in solving these issues.)

14. How would you solve this problem?
(Effective when you want to request that a person participates in a solution.)

15. My concerns are...
(Effective when you want to establish your concerns.)

16. My fears are...
(Effective when you want to establish your fears.)

17. Who has the authority to make this decision?
(Effective when you need to identify the person capable of making a decision regarding your situation.)

18. I gave myself some time to reconsider this matter. I want to change my decision.
(Effective when you are changing your mind about a situation.)

19. Can we learn something from this mistake and move on?
(Effective when you want to make this problem a learning experience.)

20. I understand what you said. I just have a different point of view.
(Effective when expressing your point of view.)

21. I need your help, please....
(Effective when you are going to ask for help.)

22. My understanding of the situation is...
(Effective when you want to express how you interpret a situation.)

23. Can you please be more patient with me? I need your patience.
*(Effective when you **need patience before you can deal with an issue**.)*

24. I don't understand what you said. Please explain...
(Effective when you need to clearly state your confusion.)

25. I will review this information and get back to you with my decision.
*(Effective when you need to stop and seek more information before **continuing to solve the problem.**)*

26. Do you have any suggestions?
(Effective when you need to establish cooperation.)

27. I will not be able to take action at this time.
(Effective when you need to clearly state that you are not in a position to take action.)

*Maintaining a priority is
as important as creating it.*

28. Let's take one point at a time.
(Effective when you need to stop and establish priorities.)

29. I want to isolate one problem at a time.
(Effective when you need to concentrate on each problem individually.)

30. We need some extra time to rethink the solutions.
(Effective when you need more time to review the information in a situation.)

31. Can you demonstrate that your solutions will be effective?
(Effective when you want a person to demonstrate the solutions to the problems.)

32. What do we need to do to resolve this conflict?
(Effective when you need to explore the help that may be necessary in solving a problem.)

33. I need to ask a favor of you, please...
(Effective when you need to set the stage for asking for someone's help.)

34. How much time do you need to solve this problem?
(Effective when you need to establish a time line in solving the problem.)

35. What do you want to see happen right now?
(Effective when you need to explore what a person wants at the moment.)

36. I am upset with _____.
(Effective when you want to express your direct dissatisfaction.)

37. I understand what you want me to do. Please allow me to explain my point of view...
(Effective when you want to politely express all points of view.)

38. Can we respectfully disagree?
(Effective when you want to express your disagreement without offending the other party.)

39. Are you willing to listen to me?
(Effective when you want to have a person listen to you.)

40. Why are you angry?
(Effective when you would like the other person to reveal what is bothering him or her.)

41. Before I answer your questions, I need to ask you for more information.
(Effective when you need additional information to understand the situation.)

42. What do you recommend we do?
(Effective when you want to empower a person to assist in solving a problem.)

43. We can't change the past; what can we do now to solve this problem?
(Effective when a person is stuck in the past and needs to move forward.)

44. Perhaps you have been misinformed.
(Effective when you believe the other person is being misguided in some way.)

45. We are not getting anywhere. Let's make this into a learning experience for both of us and focus on things we can do to move forward.
(Effective when you come to a point of no resolution.)

46. We are off course in dealing with these issues. What do we need to do to get back on track?
(Effective when we need to redirect a conversation to solving problems.)

47. How do you view this problem?
(Effective when we want to engage people in expressing their opinions.)

48. Please, I need the following things done before we move forward. Thank you.
(Effective when something needs to be done prior to moving forward.)

What we should not do can be as important as what we should do.

49. I can accommodate your request now, but in the future, please...
(*Effective when you want to accommodate someone while setting limits for the future.*)

50. I can forgive you now, but I can't allow this to happen again.
(*Effective when we can forgive someone but need to remind them that we won't allow this to happen again.*)

51. Everything is fine.
(*Effective when you wish to acknowledge that something is going well.*)

52. Is there anything else about this situation that I need to know?
(*Effective when you need to gather as much information as you can to evaluate a situation.*)

53. I know your company wants to maintain good customer relations. I need to discuss an issue with you.
(*Effective when you have a problem as a customer.*)

54. I don't understand what you are asking for. Please explain your request again.
(Effective when you are unclear about someone's request.)

55. The following points are unclear to me.
(Effective when you need clarity in a situation.)

56. Is there anything that is unclear to you?
(Effective when you want to give the other person the opportunity to clear any confusion.)

57. The choice is yours.
(Effective when you want to give the other person control in solving the issues.)

58. My decision is to...
(Effective when you want to state a clear position.)

59. What are your ideas?
(Effective when you want to engage a person in solving problems.)

60. What are your feelings about this matter?
(Effective when you want to explore a person's feelings because he or she is more comfortable with that approach.)

61. Trying to accomplish everything at one time is difficult. Let's create a step-by-step plan of action.
(Effective when you want to make an overwhelming situation more manageable.)

A mistake in life
can be a lesson to be learned.

62. What can we do now to change this situation?
(Effective when you want to give the other person the opportunity to express whatever changes he or she feels are necessary.)

63. Can I clarify my intentions?
(Effective when you need to clear up any confusion.)

64. I never intended to hurt you.
(Effective when you want to express your inner intentions.)

65. My understanding is...
(Lets people feel you are accessing a situation without taking a position.)

66. We need to have a discussion about...
(Effective when you want to explore unspoken issues.)

67. I am not prepared to answer this question at the moment because _____. (Using the word "because" is optional.)
(Effective when you want to clear any doubt about your position.)

68. It sounds like there is more to this story.
(Effective when you need more information to understand the real story.)

> *We can develop character*
> *by the crises we overcome.*

69. We need to correct this one issue.
(Effective when we need to zero in on a particular issue.)

70. Please, let's deal with the facts. Fact number one is _____.
(Effective when we need to stay focused on the facts.)

71. What is important to you?
(Effective when you want to give someone control, and the ability to express themselves.)

72. What is your number-one concern?
(Effective when you want to zero in on one concern at a time.)

73. Let's rewind a bit...you said...
(Effective when you want to reconstruct the issues.)

74. If we implement your approach, what do you think the results will be?
(Effective when you want to establish a partnership in solving the problem.)

75. We need to rethink these problems. Let's take a break and get together again. When are you available?
(Effective when you need time to rethink the problems.)

76. I am not interested in being right or wrong. I just want to solve this problem.
(Effective when you want a person to deal with the issues only.)

77. Can we note in writing what we have discussed, so that I will have a copy of our conversation?
(Effective when you want a record in writing of your conversation or agreements.)

78. You need to contact an expert in this subject matter.
(Effective when you are not qualified to answer the question or solve the problem.)

79. I would like to refer you to a person who is an authority regarding your issue.
(*Effective in redirecting someone to the proper source for help.*)

80. Do you think that yelling at me will solve this problem?
(*Effective when you want someone to stop screaming at you.*)

81. We need a plan of action to resolve this issue.
(*Effective when you want to organize a plan to resolve a matter.*)

How will we know our plan is succeeding unless we monitor it?

82. What specifically do you mean when you say the word _____?
(*Effective when you need to define the words in a conversation.*)

83. Are you aware of how you are treating me, and how it is affecting me?
(*Effective when you need to express your dissatisfaction with the way you are being treated.*)

84. You seem to be having a difficult day. Can we make another appointment to discuss your concerns?
(Effective when you want to extend some time to a person in a problem-solving situation.)

85. What evidence do you have that I said _____?
(Effective when you want to seek any evidence that you said certain statements.)

86. What evidence do you have that I did _____?
(Effective when you want to express your interest in knowing any evidence that pertains to your actions.)

87. I want to be clear about this matter. Is this what you are saying? That I _____?
(Effective when you want to clarify what the other person said.)

88. No, I won't be able to do this.
(It is effective to use the word "No" as the first word of the sentence in order to create more of an impact.)

89. Please, may I ask a favor of you?
(Effective when you need to make a request of someone.)

90. The facts suggest that...
(Effective when you want to convey your interpretation of the facts.)

91. The reality of the situation is...
(Effective when you need to state the certainty of a situation.)

92. My intentions were...
(Effective when you need to clarify the motivation for your actions.)

93. How did you arrive at this conclusion?
(Effective when you need to reconstruct the facts.)

94. My decision is final.
(Effective when you need to reveal your final position.)

Sometimes Divine Intervention is searching for ways to communicate with us.

95. We are not getting anywhere. I can contact the proper authorities regarding this particular issue. (Utilize your reference department in a local library for further information as to the proper agencies to contact.)
(Effective when someone is unwilling to cooperate toward any solution.)

96. I want to speak to the following people first.
(Effective when there were others who played a significant role in the situation.)

97. I want to inform you that I will be recording our communication in an audio or visual format so that we have documentation of this conversation.
(Effective when an organization or individual is uncooperative.)

98. Perhaps we would benefit from a male point of view.
(Effective when seeking a male point of view to better understand the factors leading to a situation.)

99. Perhaps we would benefit from a female point of view.
(Seeking a female point of view to better understand the factors leading to a situation.)

100. Do you want to resolve this issue?
(Effective when you want to establish the other person's commitment to solving the problem.)

101. In your opinion, what do we need to do to resolve this problem?
(Effective when you need to engage the other person in the problem-solving process.)

102. I believe I understand your point of view; may I explain my point of view?
(Effective when you need to establish your position in a problem.)

103. My relationship with you is important to me, and I would like to discuss an issue with you.
(Effective when you need to keep your relationship from being destroyed by a conflict.)

104. I apologize for...
(Effective when you want to take responsibility for something you did so you can move forward.)

105. I am having a hard time understanding you. Can we slow down?
(Effective when the pace of the conversation is keeping you from following the ideas.)

106. We are not getting anywhere. Would you like me to contact an investigative reporter from a local TV station regarding this issue?
(Effective with people who believe they have the power to do whatever they wish.)

107. I understand...
(Buys you some time without taking a position.)

108. I may be forced to consider legal action.
(Effective as a last option when an individual is not willing to work with you and legal action is necessary. Be certain to choose an attorney who was recommended to you and specializes in the particular issue.)

109. Can we refocus our conversation to the original subject?
(Effective when the other party has moved away from the original subject matter.)

110. Let's compare our options for solving this problem and see which is best.
(Effective when you want to compare the options for solving a problem.)

111. Let's take one step at a time.
(Effective when you need to slow the process in solving the problem and concentrate on each issue.)

112. We can cross that bridge when we come to it.
(Effective when a person is overwhelmed and needs to take a step-by-step approach.)

> *Sometimes we need to make decisions that other people may not agree with to protect our own sanity.*

113. I am not at liberty to discuss this matter with you for the following reasons...
(Effective when you want to appeal to a person's logic.)

114. I don't want to argue with you.
(Effective when you are not willing to argue.)

115. I am unable to help you. My suggestion is to...
(Effective when you want to suggest an alternative for help that you are not able to provide.)

116. I'm not qualified to answer this question.
(Effective when you want to be clear that you are not able to answer the question.)

117. Please, I need to ask a very specific question. (Pause.)
(Effective when you want to prepare a person to give you a specific answer.)

118. I would rather not discuss this issue at this time.
(Effective when you would like to exercise your right not to discuss a matter.)

119. I will call you after I complete my research.
(Effective when you need to acquire more information prior to making a decision.)

120. Please clarify some points for me.
(Effective when clarification is necessary.)

121. I believe we may have more shared interests than differences.
(Effective when you want to establish your common ground.)

122. I never meant to hurt you.
(Effective when you want to clarify that your intention was not to hurt the person you are dealing with...)

123. Silence.
(Silence makes it difficult for someone who is trying to upset you, and he or she gets an emotional payoff by doing so. Sometimes we have the right to choose what we wish to respond to. Sometimes it's not worth commenting on something, and it is best to just move on and say nothing. For example, by saying nothing we are not fueling any potential problems.)

124. What evidence do you have to support your allegations against me?
(Effective when you need to challenge the person to support untruthful claims.)

125. What will it take to resolve this matter?
(Effective when you need to motivate someone to take action in a conflict.)

126. What is really bothering you?
(Effective when you need to explore what the real issue is.)

127. I don't have an issue with you personally; I have an issue with...
(Effective when you want to separate the person from the issue.)

128. What evidence do you have to support your allegations?
(Effective when you want the other party to reveal any evidence he or she may have against you.)

129. We need to make some changes to solve this problem.
(Effective when you recognize a change is necessary to solve a problem.)

130. We need a plan to resolve this problem.
(Effective when you need to develop a plan to resolve a difficult situation.)

131. What plan of action do you suggest?
(Effective when you want to engage someone in developing a plan of action.)

132. This is my plan of action...
(Effective when you need to express your plan to resolve the issue.)

133. This is my solution...
(Effective when you want to clearly state your solution to a problem.)

134. Do you want to resolve this matter?
(Effective when you want someone to reveal his or her seriousness about resolving the matter.)

135. How can we simplify this problem?
(Effective when you believe it is necessary to simplify the matter.)

136. Can I speak to you for ten minutes without interruption?
(Effective when a person may interrupt others without being aware of doing so.)

137. Did I explain myself well enough?
(Effective when you want to be certain that you are communicating clearly.)

138. What would you like to see happen?
(Effective when you would like to engage a person into giving his or her ideas regarding a solution.)

139. My feelings are...
(Effective when you want to express how the situation is emotionally impacting you.)

140. What are your feelings regarding this situation?
(Effective when you are allowing someone to express emotions in a conflict.)

141. Do you see any opportunity to resolve this conflict?
(Effective when you want to know if a person is willing to resolve the matter.)

142. I can offer you...
(Effective when you want to state what you can give in a particular situation.)

143. I am willing to...
(Effective when you want to be clear about what you are willing to do in a particular situation.)

144. I am not willing to...
(Effective when you want to be clear about what you will not give in a situation.)

145. This is clearly a warning sign...
(Effective when you want to express the serious consequences in a given situation.)

146. This is not a priority for me at this time.
(Effective when you want to express your priorities.)

147. So what you just said is...
(Effective when you want to restate and clarify a person's response to be certain you understood it.)

148. I am not here to fight with you. Would you like to discuss the issues?
(Effective when you want to stop someone from being argumentative and to refocus on the issues.)

149. Let's try this. What do we have to lose?
(Effective when you want to encourage someone to move forward rather than do nothing.)

150. Let's try this and monitor the results.
(Effective when a person needs to have verification of his or her efforts.)

151. Life is short...Let's find a way to clean up this mess and move on.
(Effective as a call to action.)

152. Can we split the responsibilities? I will do _____ you can do that...
(*Effective when attempting to establish equal responsibilities.*)

153. I can't accept this proposal for the following reasons...
(*Effective in pointing out what you will not accept in a given proposal.*)

154. Will you reconsider talking about this?
(*Effective when approaching a person who was previously not willing to talk about a problem.*)

155. Now is not the best time for me to discuss this. Let's set up another time.
(*Effective when you want to move the discussion to a later date.*)

156. I share your concerns.
(*Effective when you want to acknowledge the other person's concerns.*)

157. Let's be realistic.
(*Effective when you want to redirect someone to discuss the reality of the situation.*)

158. I am not interested in passing judgment on anyone. I just want to resolve this matter.
(Effective when you want to focus on a resolution rather than assigning blame.)

159. Our friendship is important to me. Can we work out this problem?
(Effective when your friendship is being threatened in dealing with a conflict.)

160. I can understand how this situation could make you feel upset.
(Effective when you would like a person to know that you acknowledge his or her frustration.)

161. This question should be answered by an expert in this field.
(Effective when you want to refer a person to someone in authority to answer his or her question.)

162. I am not an expert in this field.
(Effective when you want to state that you are not qualified to deal with this problem.)

163. I am feeling very angry about _____. What can we do to resolve this problem?
(Effective when you want to express your anger and come to a resolution.)

164. The person responsible for this problem needs to be accountable.
(Effective when you want to identify the person responsible for the problem.)

165. Can we stop complaining? Let's take just one step at a time to resolve this.
(Effective when both parties are complaining with no focus on resolving the problem.)

166. Let me understand you correctly. Is this what you are saying...?
(Effective when you need to be certain about what a person is saying to you.)

167. Up until now, are you happy with the results of your decisions regarding _____? If they have not worked for you in the past, would you like to try something different?
(Effective when you want people to realize that what they have done so far has not been successful, and to encourage them to explore options.)

The way people treat others may be the way they eventually treat us.

168. Who is the right person to supply me with this answer?
(Effective when you want to identify the correct person to answer your question.)

169. Please, can I continue to talk?
(Effective when a person is cutting you off before you are finished with your explanations or responses.)

170. You are interrupting me. Can I finish what I was saying?
(Effective when someone is interrupting you and not allowing you to complete your thoughts.)

171. Are you indicating that I said _____?
(Effective when you want someone to clarify statements they allege you have made.)

172. Can you please answer my question?
(Effective when a person is not answering your question and avoiding the issue.)

173. When to say "No."
(Effective when you disagree with another person.)

174. What proof do you have that I said this?
(Effective when you want the accuser to provide evidence that you said something, particularly when you believe you didn't.)

Choose to be happy today.

175. Do we have any other options?
(Effective when you do not agree with the current plan of action and want to encourage other options.)

176. Right now, I feel you are being disrespectful to me...
(Effective when you want to make the other party aware of how you are interpreting his or her behavior in an attempt to avoid deeper conflict.)

177. What are your thoughts?
(Effective when you want to encourage the other person to engage in the problem-solving process.)

178. You are very intelligent. What are your suggestions for solving this problem?
(Effective when you want to compliment someone to encourage his or her cooperation in solving the problem.)

179. You made some excellent points. My only question is...
(Effective when you want the other person to listen to a question you have regarding the points he or she just made.)

180. Before we begin, are you willing to listen to another point of view?
(Effective in establishing whether a person will agree to listen.)

181. The reality of the situation is...
(Effective when you want to refocus on what is realistic in a situation.)

182. What can we do to prevent this problem from happening again?
(Effective when you need to prevent a problem from recurring.)

183. My suggestion is...
*(Effective **when you want to offer a helpful observation.**)*

184. What are the specific reasons for you being upset?
*(Effective **when you want to get to the root causes of the problem.**)*

185. Can we simplify this situation?
(Effective when you want to simplify the problem-solving process.)

186. I'm not prepared to make a decision at this time for the following reason...
(Effective when you are not able to make a decision for various reasons, such as you may need more facts, more time, etc.)

187. What are your thoughts about this?
(Effective when you want to engage a person in solving a problem.)

Some people recognize an opportunity,
others just pass it by.

188. Can we reconstruct what happened?
(Effective when you need to review the facts of a situation.)

189. I need to explain my actions further.
*(Effective when you need to help the other party understand the reasons for previous actions **taken.**)*

190. Do you think it's fair that you are taking this position?
(Effective when you need the other person to explore whether he or she is being fair in the position he or she has taken.)

191. What do you want to change in our approach? Be specific.
(Effective when you want to explore any changes that an individual may desire.)

192. What is unfair about what I said?
(Effective when you want the other person to explain what is unfair about your proposal.)

193. Do you think your requests are reasonable?
(Effective when you want the other person to explore whether his or her requests are reasonable.)

194. I'm having a tough day. Can I get back to you?
(Effective when you are not in a position to deal with a situation and need to put it off to a future date.)

195. Is there anything that is unclear?
(Effective when you want to confirm the other party understands the situation.)

196. How would you handle this?
(Effective when you want to engage a person in the problem-solving process.)

197. I would like to keep our friendship intact. Let's find a compromise regarding this matter.
(Effective when you want to keep your friendship in good standing in a conflicting matter.)

198. I know you are a good person. I don't have a problem with you; I just have a problem with...
(Effective when you want to separate the person from the issue.)

199. We need to look at the issue from a different perspective.
(Effective when you need to look at a problem from a different point of view.)

200. We need to stop and develop a plan to resolve this problem.
(Effective when you need a plan of action.)

201. Do you think calling me names will solve this problem?
(Effective when you want someone to become aware of his or her actions.)

202. What is stopping us from dealing with our dispute?
(Effective when you want to explore the reasons a problem is not being solved.)

203. I am frustrated about...
(Effective when you want to express your frustrations in a matter.)

204. My suggestion is...
(Effective when you want to make a helpful suggestion.)

205. What are the specific reasons causing you to be upset?
(Effective when you want to know why a person is getting upset.)

206. I need to reexamine the facts.
(Effective when you want to reevaluate the facts in the matter.)

207. It would be unethical to do this...
(Effective when you want to express your moral point of view as a factor.)

208. We need to reopen the lines of communication between us.
(Effective when you want to reestablish communication with someone.)

209. If you're angry about something, let's talk about it so we can resolve it.
(*Effective in allowing people to express their unspoken anger or resentment.*)

210. Thank you for notifying me about this problem.
(*Effective when you want to immediately acknowledge a person's problem.*)

211. What solution would allow us both to benefit?
(*Effective when you want to benefit in a situation and allow the other person to benefit also.*)

212. What do you mean by _____?
(*Effective when you want to know what a person means by using certain words.*)

213. What is your perception of the problem?
(*Effective when you allow the other person to express his or her point of view.*)

214. I am sorry you interpreted it that way—what I meant was...
(*Effective when what you said was misinterpreted.*)

215. I did my best...
(*Effective when you want someone to know you made the effort to do the best you could.*)

216. Given how severe the problem is, this is my solution...
(Effective when you want to implement a much-needed solution.)

217. Do you think getting professional help will aid us?
(Effective when you see the necessity for professional help.)

218. Are you okay? Can I do anything to help you?
(Effective when you want to show concern for a person who is strongly upset but gives no indication of being physically aggressive.)

219. I will look into this matter.
(This phrase will buy you some time to look into this matter, but it also gives the other person the confidence that you are dealing with the issue.)

220. My question is: Is this your problem or mine?
(We sometimes don't stop to think about who owns the problem. Some people would have us believe that the problem is ours when he or she will not accept the responsibility for solving it.)

REMEMBER,

YOU HAVE THE OPTION TO SAY "I DON'T WANT TO DISCUSS THIS MATTER ANY FURTHER," WHICH KEEPS A PERSON FROM DISCUSSING THE ISSUE ANY LONGER.

WHAT TO SAY WHEN TRYING TO BE FAIR

"TO BE FAIR TO BOTH OF US LET'S..."

Simplicity can be profound.

Examples are sometimes what we need to hear.... "I heard what you have to say.... But please give me an example of what you are talking about."

*Admitting you don't know
something is better than saying
something you don't know.*

*Sometimes the farther we are
removed from something the
clearer it becomes.*

*When a letter can make a
difference...*
    *There are things that can be
    said in a letter that we may
    not be able to communicate
    personally to someone....
sending a letter may re-open
the pathway of communication.*

> ## "What we are aware of we are responsible for."
> **Kenneth R. Petrucci, MSW**

Do you have something you need to make a note of? If so, write it down so you don't forget it.

_____

_____

_____

_____

_____

_____

_____

> ## "Some people who are obsessed with being in control may have a problem with being out of control."
> **Kenneth R. Petrucci, MSW**

LIFE-CHANGING MENTAL GYMNASTICS

In preparing our minds for a successful day, we can choose our state of mind. Before you begin your day slowly and convincingly repeat aloud these self-motivation phrases seven times.

1. Today I choose to have a confident state of mind.

2. Today I choose to be grateful for what I have.

3. Today I choose to have no one affect my peace of mind.

4. Today I choose to have a happy state of mind.

5. Today I choose to have victory over any obstacles.

6. Today I choose to make decisions that are beneficial to my wellbeing.

7. Today I choose to take responsibility for my actions.

8. Today I choose to learn the lessons my mistakes are trying to teach me.

Insights into Assertiveness Skills

- Sometimes it's not what we say but the **manner** in which we say it. Our tone of voice, aura, body language, and emotions can be vehicles of communication.
- Let's gather our thoughts and take a moment to say what we truly **think and feel**.
- Listen with a **nonjudgmental** attitude.
- When saying **"no,"** use it at the beginning of the sentence. It avoids the possibility of developing anxiety about saying **"no."**
- Select an **environment** that aids us in being comfortable in discussing our points.
- Remember, **human nature** dictates that we are asking ourselves this one question: "What's in it for me?" Appeal to a person's wants and needs whenever possible.
- Remember, some people need to **experience** more of life before they can understand what we are saying.
- Some people need to take the time to **reflect** upon what was said before they can understand it.
- Some people need a **less forceful** approach when we are being assertive with them.
- Remember, some people want **empathy** first, then problem solving second.

- Sometime it is best **not to respond** verbally to people when they are being difficult. Some people get an emotional payoff by seeing us losing our cool.

> *"A mistake requires us to take corrective actions to eliminate the problem from recurring."*
>
> **Kenneth R. Petrucci, MSW**

*LETTING GO...*Sometimes we need to let go of something to create room for something else.

*BEING HONEST...*Being honest with ourselves is one of the biggest challenges in life.

Being honest with ourselves is one of the first steps to resolving problems in life.

Are you sometimes dishonest with yourself?

Yes _____ No _____ Somewhat _____

Indirect Communication vs. Direct Communication

EXAMPLES OF INDIRECT COMMUNICATION	EXAMPLES OF DIRECT COMMUNICATION
1. It seems like I am always being taken advantage of.	✓ Please treat me with the respect I deserve.
2. Our money problems are getting bigger and bigger.	✓ Can you stop spending money on some of the items you may not need?
3. I seem to be doing all the work.	✓ Can we divide the responsibilities?
4. I can't seem to get anyone to help me with my problems.	✓ Please listen to my problems. Maybe you can give me some good advice.

5. It's been awhile since you borrowed my book.	✓ How much more time do you need to borrow my book?
6. Our relationship is always in trouble.	✓ Can we sit down to discuss our relationship issues?
7. You seem to be angry all the time.	✓ Are you angry about something?
8. There is no way I am driving this car.	✓ I am not driving this car because it appears to be unsafe.
9. I never heard from you.	✓ Is there a reason you have not been calling me?
10. I can't seem to find friends to travel with.	✓ Are you interested in traveling with me?

Use direct communication by taking a moment, gathering your thoughts, and then saying what you truly think and feel.

Confrontation vs. Cooperation

The following are examples of confrontation versus cooperation approaches to dealing with difficult behavior.

Confrontation
1. The way you spoke to my sister last night was disrespectful.

Cooperation
The way you spoke to my sister last night upset her. I would suggest trying a less intense approach when talking with her about her college grades. A more laid-back approach would be great, because she gets insecure at times.

Confrontation
2. Stop implying that I did something wrong.

Cooperation
Do you believe that I have done something wrong?

Confrontation
3. How can I lose weight if you keep offering me chocolate chip cookies?

Cooperation

I am cutting back on sugar because of my weight-loss program. Please stop offering me those great chocolate chip cookies.

Confrontation

4.   I want you to accept the return of my shirt right now.

Cooperation

What is your return policy?

Confrontation

5.   This marriage is over if you can't control your spending.

Cooperation

Our budget is off. We can't pay our bills because of some credit card bills you acquired. What can we do to resolve this problem?

Confrontation

6.   Stop calling me. You are driving me crazy.

Cooperation

I won't be buying a car from you. Please stop calling me.

Confrontation

7.   I want this car fixed correctly this time.

Cooperation

I am having the same problem with my car. Can you fix this problem so it won't happen again?

Confrontation

8.   I paid my taxes. Why are you always sending me bills?

Cooperation

I have a receipt that indicates that I have paid my taxes up to date. Can you tell me why I am receiving another tax bill?

Confrontation

9.   You are always calling me about my son's behavior.

Cooperation

This is the third time I was asked to speak with my son's teacher. What can we do to prevent these problems from occurring again?

Confrontation

10. Keep the car moving, buddy.

Cooperation

Please continue to move forward.

Study the above differences between the confrontation and cooperation dialogue.

For My Cherished Reader:

Do you have people in your life that you would like to express your appreciation to? If so, make a note of the individuals and decide to express your gratitude to these individuals while they are still alive.

1 _____

2 _____

3 _____

4 _____

5 _____

6 _____

7 _____

8 _____

9 _____

10 _____

How to Improve Your Listening Skills

Good listening begins with having an open mind.

Remember...not interrupting when someone is speaking is also a part of listening.

1. **Secure an environment** that creates the **atmosphere to concentrate on the conversation.**
2. <u>Listen</u> to what the person is saying rather than thinking about your response to his or her comments.
3. Focus on the facts.
4. Allow a person enough time to speak.
5. Place yourself in his or her shoes when necessary.
6. Show concern in your body language when necessary.
7. Focus on the person. Make him or her feel special.
8. If something is unclear, ask the person to explain it.
9. Work on making someone feel comfortable if you are trying to establish an open conversation.
10. If you are confused, repeat what the person is saying to clarify whether you heard it correctly.

11. Using your body language, let the person know you are listening to him or her. An example would be expressing your interest with your eyes and a slight nod of the head.
12. Review the facts with the listener.

How to Control Your Anger

1. Take a written inventory of what makes you angry.
2. When those potentially anger-inducing issues begin to surface, recognize them and try to find an effective way to deal with them before any become a crisis. If you can't control yourself, consider redirecting your thoughts and actions.
   a. Do something physical that you enjoy.
   b. Call a friend to get your mind off your anger issues and change your mood, or discuss your issues with a resourceful friend who may help you.
   c. Redirect your mind by doing something you enjoy, such as playing video games, doing crossword puzzles, or listening to your favorite music, etc.
   d. Take a deep breath and relax.
   e. Practice The Inner Peace Relaxation Technique which is in this book.

   Remember that it is important to occupy our minds with something that replaces the stressful patterns. An example is that it is difficult to laugh and cry at the same time.

The Kenneth R. Petrucci, MSW, Inner Peace Relaxation Technique

Using this relaxation technique involves **focused** concentration; therefore, **refrain** from activities such as driving a car, using machinery, etc.

The Kenneth R. Petrucci Inner Peace Relaxation Technique, created by the author, is as follows:

(Be sure to read all of the following steps before beginning this procedure.)

> ➢ Before you begin your relaxation technique, you can **draw a circle,** place a dot in the center, and concentrate on the dot for a period of time. This technique may help you become focused before you begin your relaxation session. The length of time that this technique can be practiced is at your discretion.
> ➢ If you can, close your eyes.
> ➢ Begin by briefly shaking your hands to release tension.
> ➢ Sit with the palms of your hands facing up to the ceiling.
> ➢ Take a moment and visualize a peaceful scene for a desired period of time. Now slowly inhale

this feeling of peace and slowly exhale any stressful emotions for a desired period of time. Repeat the process until you experience a feeling of relaxation. Remember, once you experience this feeling of relaxation, it becomes easier to achieve it again. You may practice this technique for the length of time that you feel is necessary.

While using this technique you can incorporate one of the following to assist you in your relaxation experience:
1. Noise-blocking headphones or earplugs
2. Relaxing music

Special Note:
Kenneth R. Petrucci, MSW taught a relaxation exercise to law enforcement personnel at the Rhode Island Municipal Police Academy.

How to Deal with an Angry Person

- General Guide -

1. In general, keep a comfortable **distance** between you and an angry person.
2. If you are standing, **encourage the other person to sit down with you.**
3. Lower the **tone** of your voice.
4. Allow the person to **vent** by letting him or her speak. Later, you may want to consider asking what is specifically bothering the person.
5. Remain **calm.** If you're upset, it will only encourage the angry person to be more upset.
6. Consider **leaving** the area if the situation has the potential of escalating into violence.
7. When necessary, be **firm.**
8. Be **decisive.**
9. Be **brief.**
10. When appropriate, consider expressing your **sympathy.**
11. When appropriate, we can consider explaining the fact that we can **feel** someone's pain because we have experienced a similar situation.
12. When necessary, create **structure** in dealing with the angry person.

13. When necessary, explain the **consequences** of the person's negative behavior.
14. Set a **time** period to establish a plan to resolve these problems.
15. **Monitor** your plan for success.

> *"Human beings can be the person they want to be, the person they pretend to be, or the person they truly are."*
>
> **Kenneth R. Petrucci, MSW**

How to Deal with Coworkers When They become Difficult

- ➢ Recognize the subjects that **trigger** the difficulty in a coworker.
- ➢ If possible, try to avoid non-work-related **meetings** during which some coworkers may routinely become difficult.
- ➢ If you need to be assertive with a coworker, review and consider using one of the 220 **persuasive phrases** to use when responding to a person who is being difficult.
- ➢ Take **responsibility** for your involvement in these conflicts.
- ➢ **Clarify** the fact that your coworker understands your comments.
- ➢ Develop a **plan** of action that prevents this difficult situation from happening again.
- ➢ Decide when a person's difficult behavior is **beyond** being resolved.
- ➢ Remember what **triggered** this difficult situation.

> *"Admitting we have a problem is the first step to solving it."*
>
> **Kenneth R. Petrucci, MSW**

Do you know people that would benefit from reading this book? If so, please list the individuals and let them know about this self-improvement book.

1._____

2._____

3._____

4._____

5._____

6._____

7._____

8._____

9._____

10._____

11. _____

12. _____

13. _____

14. _____

15. _____

KEEP THE LINES OF COMMUNICATION OPEN...

Some suicides may be the result of believing that one does not have any other options except to take one's own life. Sometimes medications may help an individual to improve his or her mental health condition. The use of various forms of therapy may assist such a person managing a mental health issue. **Also, remaining close to people or counselors and keeping the lines of communication open better enables a counselor, friend or relative to become aware of the condition, and bring the depression into the open so that help may be sought before the situation becomes a crisis.**

In the end it is important to remember that ALL of us may one day need the help that is necessary to cope with life.

Do you keep your lines of communication open with family, friends, doctors, counselors, etc.?

Yes_____ No_____ Somewhat_____

Strategies to Effectively Deal with a Variety of Bosses

*Best approaches to utilize when dealing with different styles of management. Remember, a boss is a **human being** with all the personal issues and the positive potential of any human being. A boss has a responsibility to carry out an agenda that may not appeal to us, or of which we may not be aware.*

A. The Authoritative Manager
Employees' strategies:
- Be direct.
- Be brief.
- Be less confrontational.
- Be accountable.
- Offer clear solutions.
- Compliment the boss's successful procedures.
- Try not to criticize your boss's inadequacies unless you are willing to put your job status on the line.

B. The Collaborative Manager
Employees' strategies:
- Offer your ideas for improvement.

- Try to keep a good working relationship with coworkers.
- Indicate that you are available if necessary.

C. **The Laid-Back Manager**
Employees' strategies:
- Be as relaxed as possible.
- Take your time to explain your points.

D. **The Self-Destructive Manager**
Employees' strategies:
- Be specific; focus on facts rather than personalities or vague ideas.
- Give credit to a boss when it is deserved.
- Agree with your boss whenever you can if you feel he or she is impossible to work with.
- If the issues with your boss become impossible because he or she is unjustifiably trying to hurt you in a personal way, it may be necessary to bring in a supervisor or union representative as a witness.

E. **"Fair and balanced" management style**
Employee's strategy:
- If your manager is fair and balanced toward you, just be yourself and be mutually fair and balanced toward your manager.

NOTE: Mr. Petrucci has been an employee and also managed other people.

How Bosses Can Deal with the Difficult Behaviors of Their Employees

Remember to monitor any of your plans of action to determine your results.

1. First, **listen** to your employees. Focus on what they are saying rather than what you are thinking.
2. Being **approachable** to your employees allows them to feel that they can ask for help or instructions to accomplish the best job possible.
3. Decide what the **real** issues are by saying, with a non-assuming attitude, "I have an issue with…, why is this happening?"
4. Decide who is **responsible** for this problem.
5. State how this problem will be **prevented** from happening again.
6. Decide if **disciplinary** actions are necessary.
7. In general, it is best not to be **overly friendly** with your employees because it may become difficult to make a request of them, or to fire an employee, although

many different styles of management may work for some managers.

8. Give **equal** treatment to all employees.
9. Acknowledge your position of **authority**.
10. When it is necessary to take a **position**, take it without feeling guilty.
11. Whenever necessary, **demonstrate** your request.
12. Create a **system** to monitor your employees' completed task(s).
13. As a manager, try not to attack an employee because of your own **personal issues**.
14. Try to find a lesson to be **learned** by resolving the problem.

"Remember—sometimes it is good to question authorities; sometimes they are incorrect."

Kenneth R. Petrucci, MSW

WHEN THE MATTER MUST REMAIN CONFIDENTIAL...SAY:
"I AM UNABLE TO DISCUSS THIS MATTER AS IT MUST REMAIN CONFIDENTIAL."

How to Be Effective When Making a Complaint

❖ Be **clear** in your request, using as many facts as possible.

❖ Ask to speak to a person with the **authority** to resolve your problem.

❖ Try to be **diplomatic** in your initial request.

❖ If diplomacy isn't working, it's time to be **firm** in your position.

❖ If you're right but no resolution is in the making, it's time to ask for the **supervisor**.

❖ If no resolution is proposed, it's time to ask for a **regional supervisor** or **CEO** of the organization. The higher up you appeal in management, the more authority that person will have to resolve your problem.

❖ You can file a complaint in writing using registered mail and requesting a **return** receipt to be signed.

❖ If no resolution has been accomplished, bring your letter to the Better Business Bureau and the proper authorities who may regulate or license the business or agency you are complaining about. Examples of the authorities can be found in your city, state, or federal government. Ask a reference librarian to assist you in finding the appropriate agency to contact. Remind the organization or business that we are in an age of social media and if a resolution is not found, you may post the negative experience on many sites viewed by potential customers looking for the company's products or services. Remember to **verify** your information as being **factual**.

❖ **Recognize** what you will not negotiate.

❖ Recognize when it is necessary to consider a **compromise**.

❖ Work hard at gathering any **documentation** for your complaint, such as photos, videos, or printed materials; documentation may give you the edge you need to be successful in your complaint.

    a) When you are speaking with the person who will actually be handling the issue be sure to write down his or her name and ask for his or her contact information and company identification number;

    b) Ask if your problem-solving procedures will have a confirmation or reference number. If a number does exist, write it down;

    c) Also, write down the date and the time of the discussion;

    d) Ask the person who is handling the problem for a time or day this problem will be resolved.

    e) When returning to resolve the problem be sure to indicate the person's name you want to speak with, the date and time that you spoke with the person and the confirmation number.

Handling Difficulties When
Returning an Item

1. Indicate to the business representative that you would like to return your item and state your **reasons.**
2. If no cooperation is forthcoming, ask to speak with the manager on duty. Explain your **issues** to the manager.
3. If the reply is unacceptable to you, then ask for the name and **contact information** of the president or owner of the company.
4. If the representative does not have that information, make him or her aware that you will obtain the name of the president or owner of the company and that you will be filing a **complaint.**
5. If no resolution is made, create a **timeline** to resolve these issues.

"Change can be an opportunity for growth."

Kenneth R. Petrucci, MSW

EFFECTIVE PREPARATION WHEN CONSULTING AN ATTORNEY

Seek an attorney who is experienced and proficient in your area of concern and who may offer a free initial consultation. Also, all contacts the attorney may have can possibly be used to your benefit. You may wish to contact your state's Bar Association to request an attorney who works with your particular matter, and to obtain information.

Any research that you conduct online regarding the general laws of your state as they relate to your issue may help you to better understand your situation as it relates to the law. Also, you may wish to visit or call your local state law library to conduct any research regarding your legal issue. In general, another resource may be your local reference librarian who can be of assistance to you.

Before the initial meeting with the attorney, be prepared by having with you, in writing, the accurate facts of your matter and specifically what you wish to accomplish. In the event that the attorney is requesting a retainer fee, be certain that you clarify with the attorney the amount of his or her retainer fee and the reason for this fee, as well as the hourly fee. Also, you may wish to consider a Contingent Fee Agreement with the attorney. Per The American Bar Association "a client pays a contingent fee only if the lawyer handles a case successfully." Periodically ask for an itemized statement of the work the attorney has done and the cost.

Request from the attorney his or her proposals for resolving your matter. Be certain to emphasize to the attorney that communication with him or her is of the utmost importance to you.

Any professional, such as an attorney, is licensed. Therefore, in the event that you have an issue with the attorney's services or conduct, you can contact the Bar Association in your state to discuss your issue. The mission of the American Bar Association is to "...promote competence, ethical conduct and professionalism." (American Bar Association, Mission, Goal 2). You may retain a highly skillful attorney, however in the U.S.A. you can terminate your representation at any time regardless of any fee agreement you signed. If you have chosen to hire a particular attorney, seek opinions from those you respect about the particular lawyer or conduct online research from clients who have used that attorney. Plus you can check the disciplinary history of any attorney in most states by contacting the local disciplinary office of attorneys.

Before entering into a lawsuit, consider the benefits and the costs of the suit. Remember, although the attorney may indicate that it is difficult to determine the exact amount of the cost of the lawsuit you certainly can ask what the approximate highest expense will be. Remember that anger and emotions can motivate you into entering into a lawsuit or continuing a lawsuit that may not benefit you.

As in any profession, when an attorney's work is effectively done we truly appreciate his or her services.

An alternative option to hiring an attorney may be to consider mediation for your particular matter. Mediation is utilizing the services of a mediator, who is an impartial third party, to resolve your issue. To find a local mediator contact your reference librarian in your state for organizations or the names of mediators who may assist you.

Finally, if you are representing yourself in a lawsuit consider these main points if you must appear in court:

1. Be brief.
2. Document the facts.
3. Be specific.
4. Say no more than is necessary because saying what is unnecessary may complicate matters for you.

How to Deal with Difficult Behavior When Solving Marital or Personal Relationship Issues

1. Remember, to set a stage for better listening, take the time to listen with a **nonjudgmental** attitude.
2. Try to **place** yourself in the other person's position while listening.
3. Focus on the person by using your body language to express your **interest** in what is being discussed.
4. Try to identify the **real** issues, which may not be so apparent, by mutually agreeing to be open and honest with each other about your concerns.
5. Remember, what is **unimportant** to you may be very important to another person.
6. Try to develop a **plan** that will solve your problems.
7. If necessary, set **smaller** workable goals.
8. Set deadlines to **monitor** the success of your smaller goals.
9. Be willing to **establish** ways to prevent these problems from happening again.

10. If necessary, involve an effective **third-party** person such as a good friend or relative to help resolve the issues.
11. Seek **counseling** if necessary.
12. Consider a **support** group when necessary.

"Why be confrontational when cooperation would have been successful?"

Kenneth R. Petrucci, MSW

Secretly needing a hug ...

From early childhood we were given hugs to comfort us. As we age we sometimes feel hugs are a form of stress relief for children, but stored in our long term memory and subconscious mind is the established association of hugs reduce stress. Do you know someone who may secretly need a hug today?

Twelve Reasons Friendships Begin to Fail

1. If we frequently take more of a friend's **time** than they have available our friend may begin to avoid us.
2. We are always focusing on what is best for **us** in a friendship.
3. We don't deal with **why** our friendship is in trouble. If a friend seems upset with us, a simple approach is saying, **"Is something bothering you in our friendship? If so, do you want to discuss it?"**
4. We don't create a **good environment** in which **to discuss** our conflicts with our friends.
5. We don't consider what we can do to keep our friendships **intact**. We sometimes make an issue of everything in our friendships.
6. We don't **apologize** when we are wrong in dealing with our friendships.
7. We don't understand our friends' **limitations**. We sometimes place our friends in stressful situations because of not considering their limitations. We sometimes forget that we all have limitations.
8. When necessary, we overlook the need to be **honest** with our friends.

9. We periodically **forget** to keep in touch with our friends.
10. In discussing our friendship problems, we sometimes are not able to **identify** the real issues.
11. We don't take the time to **listen** to our friends.
12. We forget that **loyalty and respect** for our friends is of the utmost importance.

"It's important to know our limitations as well as our possibilities."
Kenneth R. Petrucci, MSW

Some mistakes I have made in my life and the lessons I have learned: A time for reflection.

MISTAKE:

Lesson Learned:

MISTAKE:

Lesson Learned:

MISTAKE:

Lesson Learned:

MISTAKE:

Lesson Learned:

MISTAKE:

Lesson Learned:

Family Issues (Including Interacting with Relatives)

1. Family issues can be complex because of the emotional **interconnected** aspect of families in general. We will sometimes try to extend ourselves to just keep peace among family members.

2. In the beginning of resolving a family issue, look into one matter. Is there one family member who has more **influence** in general with the family? Is there one member who is a peacemaker? Is there one member who is knowledgeable about your matter of concern? First, try to meet with members individually who are influential or peacemakers or knowledgeable about your issues. Later, arrange to meet with all the members of the family.

3. Select an **environment** that aids you in discussing your family issues.

4. Sometimes family members need to hear that you **care** for them, but you may still need to take a certain position.

5. Family members will be looking for **fairness** in group meetings.

6. The word **respect** can be a big issue in family meetings. Some members feel they require more respect simply because of their ages.

7. Try to note and remember **what works** in dealing with certain family members. Try to note and remember what does not work.

8. There are times when it seems impossible to communicate your ideas because some members refuse or are unable to accept different points of view. These members may have their own personal issues that limit them. It is **your reaction** to people that you have control of. Sometimes you have no choice but to just state your ideas briefly and focus on the facts.

9. If yelling occurs, you can **repeat these phrases**: "Do you think that yelling will solve anything? If you continue to yell, I will leave."

10. Sometimes a conflict in a meeting is beyond repair at that time. It may be necessary to take a **time-out** and return when emotions are calmer.

> *"The only way we can make a change is by being willing to make changes."*
>
> **Kenneth R. Petrucci, MSW**

How Elderly People Can Deal with Difficult Behavior

1. Inform people if you have any limitations such as **physical or medical challenges.**
2. Break down your problems into workable, **smaller** goals.
3. Set **limits** with people when necessary.
4. Consider reviewing and using the **220 prepared phrases** to use when responding to a person who is being difficult.
5. If a senior citizen is experiencing abuse, he or she can inform their family, a relative, a friend, the Police Department or the **Department of Elderly Affairs** in his or her state.
6. If a person is known to be difficult, it may be necessary to have a **friend** with you to keep this person in control.
7. Keep **informed** about any information necessary in dealing with your difficult situation. An example may be your need to be assertive regarding a medical procedure. Therefore, you may need to read, search the Internet, and/or consult with a specialist so that you will have more input regarding the most effective approach to your problem.

8. **Network** with agencies that provide resources that can help you deal with problematic issues.

9. A senior citizen may need to ask for help from their family, a friend or a relative. As we grow older, it may be necessary to ask for some **extra assistance**.

10. There is no need to feel **embarrassed** about asking for help from family, friends or relatives. As we grow older, we will all need some extra assistance..

11. Work at keeping yourself in the **best physical and mental condition** possible to be strong enough to handle adversity.

> *"We can't control the world, but we can control the quality of our thoughts."*
>
> **Kenneth R. Petrucci, MSW**

How Children Can Deal with the Difficult Behavior of Other Classmates

✓ **Identify the issues** that trigger difficult behavior in your classmates. Stay away from these issues.

✓ In general, try to become aware of an **issue** before it becomes a larger and more difficult problem to handle.

✓ If necessary, consider reviewing and using the **prepared phrases** in this book.

✓ Remember to avoid trying to be **accepted** by every classmate. Overly seeking acceptance can lead to participating in negative group activities in which you otherwise would not choose to participate.

✓ Stand tall; appear **confident**.

✓ Develop a supportive **network** with students who are interested in doing well in school.

✓ If you can't resolve these difficult situations, it may be necessary to clearly state your problem to a **school administrator**.

✓ If necessary, seek **counsel** with your parent(s), other relatives, friends, or a counselor at school or in private practice.

Remember, some of your classmates may be continually getting into trouble. It is important to realize if you are associating with classmates who are continually in trouble you may find yourself unconsciously mimicking their disturbing behavior.

> *"When we die, our past, present, and future may become one."*
>
> **Kenneth R. Petrucci, MSW**

In your life, what do you value more than money?
(Write your answers here.)

How Parents Can Deal with the Difficult Behavior of Their Children

1. Select an **environment** that creates privacy to allow your child to feel comfortable enough to open up.
2. If necessary, seek more **information** related to your problem area.
3. Identify the **real issues** by asking your child to be open and honest with you.
4. Initially, assure your child that he or she may come to you with **any** problem and that you will listen with a **nonjudgmental** attitude.
5. Identify what **responsibility** your child has in this problem.
6. Identify what responsibility **anyone else** may have in this problem.
7. Create a **plan** to solve this problem.
8. **Monitor** the success of your plan.
9. If necessary, seek **counseling** for you or your child.
10. It is important to **always** remind your child that you love him or her but that you need to discuss a specific issue. Remember, do not assume that you know what your child is thinking. Always inform your child of the importance of keeping the lines of communication open between you. However, be **consistent** in your support, consequences, or punishments.

How to Deal with Your Parents When They Become Upset with You

1. In general, make an attempt to sit down which hopefully will encourage your parents to sit down so that you will both be on an equal level, therefore not intimidating each other.
2. Try to have your parents express specifically why they are upset with you. Use phrases such as, "Why are you upset with me?"
3. Be sure you understand the reasons they are upset. Use phrases such as, "Are you upset with me because I _____?"
4. If your parents are yelling you can lower your voice to help reduce the angry atmosphere.
5. Learn to accept responsibility for your actions.
6. If the problem becomes unmanageable, it may be necessary to take a break and return later to solve the problem.
7. Sometimes it is necessary to have a third-party person such as a friend, relative or professional mental health counselor to help in solving your problem with your parents.

8. Remember, your parents may have personal stressors (for example, money issues) that may have nothing to do with you and of which you may not be aware. Their stress factors could be partly why they are upset.
9. Acting respectfully toward your parents will make it easier for you and them to resolve the problem.
10. If child abuse exists you can contact your local child protective services in your state or inform your local Police Department, family, a relative, or a friend about your child abuse.

"Sometimes what we are seeking in life we already have."

Kenneth R. Petrucci, MSW

A Teacher's Guide to Resolving Behavior Problems

1. Whenever possible, create a more **private** environment when discussing your problems with a student. An example would be in the hallway or rear of the room. This will avoid a student being affected by other classmates while you are talking.

2. Let the student know that you can **resolve** these issues now, or have their parents come to school to resolve these issues. Indicate that these are the two choices. Ask the student which approach they want to use. Remember, if students feel it is their decision to do something, they are more likely to accept it. Incidentally, every student I have counseled chose to deal with his or her problem individually rather than having the parents called in.

3. Identify the **real issues,** which may not be so obvious. Be specific in your exploration of the real issues. In a non-threatening voice use phrases such as "Let's be honest with each other." Then pause and ask, "What is upsetting you?"

4. Set a **plan** in place to resolve these issues using small, workable goals.

5. Set **deadlines** to resolve these problem areas.

6. **Monitor** the success of your plan to resolve these issues.

7. Be willing to **change** the course of resolution when necessary.

8. Involve your **supervisor** or **principal** when necessary.

9. Involve **parents** or **counselors** when necessary.

10. I worked at various grade levels – elementary, middle and high school, as a school psychotherapist. When I was working with elementary school children I would ask a child this specific question: "What do you want to be when you grow up?" Whatever his or her choice was helped me to motivate the child because we would explore his or her career choice. We would paste any pictures or drawings that we made of the possible future profession in notebooks, and he or she would visualize himself or herself in that field. Also, we would discuss what his or her profession does and why this would make them happy. This approach was very successful for me because it allowed a student to begin developing an identity that he or she became excited about. Their motivation to attain a preferred profession would affect their desire to attend school in order to achieve their goals. Regardless of the student's age, this technique was always effective. Do not hesitate at any grade level (elementary, middle or high school) to get a student involved in a career that he or she chooses. Doing so can be a motivating factor for the student to acquire

the education necessary to achieve career goals. This process will facilitate building a foundation on the student's desires. In conclusion, the educational system waits until later to conduct career counseling. My experiences with students indicate that we should **start** as soon as early **childhood**.

Remember...

My suggestion is to begin every class with having students of any age **draw a circle, place a dot in the center of the circle, and concentrate on the dot** to gain focus before classes begin. This technique can also be used in problematic situations in which a student may need to focus before you discuss his or her problems.

Also, at the beginning of the school year have students decide on a **career**, however young they are, and place on their desk the name of the **profession** and keep it there from the first day of class to the end of the year. **Remind students that the career they have chosen can be obtained by doing well in school.**

> *"A good friend is like an insurance policy against life's tragedies."*
> **Kenneth R. Petrucci, MSW**

A Formula to Handle Customer Complaints

- Express **concerns** for the customer's complaint by repeating statements such as "I understand how you can be frustrated."
- Listen with a **nonjudgmental** attitude.
- Allow the customer enough **time** to explain his or her complaints.
- **Repeat** the complaints to be sure you heard them correctly, such as, "So what you're saying is _____. Is this correct?" This allows the customer to know he or she has been truly heard by you, and also to hear the content of what he or she just said. If the customer's statement was unreasonable, this will often be realized by him or her at this stage.
- Apply a **plan** to resolve the issue.
- If necessary **monitor** your plan of action.

Remember to make an attempt to resolve your customer complaint as quickly as possible in order not to fuel the customer's complaint any longer.

> *"The time we spend complaining about a problem could have been used to solve it."*
>
> Kenneth R. Petrucci, MSW

Do you avoid trying to solve your own problems?

Yes _____ No _____ Somewhat _____

A Salesperson's Guide to a Customer's Concern (including a simplified sales system)

1. Spend the **time** to identify the **real** issue that the customer is concerned about.

2. Isolate the customer's **concerns** using statements such as, "Please specifically tell me what concerns you." *(Pause and give the customer enough time to think and respond.)*

3. Come to an **agreement** on how this issue will be handled using statements such as, "If we were to resolve your concern in this way, would you like to own this product or enjoy the benefits of our service?"

Remember

A customer's unspoken issue with you, your product or your service can cost you sales; therefore, it is important to you and the customer to resolve these concerns or objections. Remember that some of the best salespeople in the world **speak less and listen more.**

"Dreams are sometimes letters sent to us from our subconscious minds."

Kenneth R. Petrucci, MSW

The Simplified Sales System

1. *Ask the customer to explain the need for your product or service.*
   Sample question – "Why do you feel you need....?"

2. *Explain slowly and clearly the benefits of the item or service.*

3. *Ask if there are any concerns about the merchandise or service.*
   Sample question - "Do you have any concerns about....?"

4. *In a relaxed manner, ask the customer if he or she would like to make the purchase.*

Remember, represent a product or service that you believe in because it radiates in your sale's dialogue. Also, you may truly help a person by utilizing your product or service. I developed the above system of selling from having a previous award-winning successful career as a salesman.

Spend less time debating a solution and more time implementing it.

Checklist for Evaluating Your Approach after Dealing with a Person Who Has Become Difficult

1) Did I obtain enough **facts** or **information** before approaching this difficult situation?
   _____ Yes _____ Somewhat _____ No

2) Was **I specific** enough in my discussions?
   _____ Yes _____ Somewhat _____ No

3) Did I create a **timeline** to follow through on the predetermined goals?
   _____ Yes _____ Somewhat _____ No

4) Did I establish **preventative** measures to keep this difficult situation from occurring again?
   _____ Yes _____ Somewhat _____ No

5) Did I accept **responsibility** for my role in this difficult situation?
   _____ Yes _____ Somewhat _____ No

Kenneth R. Petrucci, MSW, Answers Questions about Difficult Behavior

Q. Can a person inherit personality traits?
A. Yes. Sometimes we inherit personality traits that can develop into difficult patterns of behavior. If this is the case, it's important to recognize when people are having difficulties with us and the reasons for those difficulties. Work to modify those particular traits.

Q. Can a person's secrets cause him or her to be difficult?
A. Yes. If a person is struggling with personal issues, they may appear to be difficult, but it's the inner struggle with these issues that creates the difficult behavior.

Q. Why are some people rude?
A. When a person lashes out to offend others, he or she may be suffering from personal issues or insecurities, or simply may not know that what he or she is doing is affecting people in a negative manner.

Q. Can a person's parents contribute to a person being difficult?

A. Yes. Sometimes we unconsciously mimic our parents' difficult behavior patterns because when we were children they were the central figures in our lives.

> *"Sometimes saying nothing stops us from fueling a confrontation."*
>
> **Kenneth R. Petrucci, MSW**

Q. How do you deal with spouses when they become difficult?

A. The very first task is to identify the issues that are creating the difficulties. Next step is to isolate the most important issues. It is important to identify a common issue that you and your spouse consider the primary issue to deal with. Begin with the most important issue first, then the second most important issue, and so on. Before you explore your problems together **agree** to a mutual goal. Be honest with yourselves. Decide as a couple what you are able to do differently to resolve your problem. Establish a mutually convenient time to discuss your issues and continue to re-establish your next meeting time. Also, remind your spouse of the positive aspects of your marriage, and that all marriages face some negative issues at times.

Be open to early counseling when necessary and realize that counselors are initially not always a good fit. Therefore, you may need to explore different counselors to find the correct counselor for you and your spouse.

Please refer to the section in the subject matters titled "The Kenneth Petrucci Self-help Information Process" which will assist you to discover the reasons for your behavior.

Q. How do you deal with a friend who is being difficult?
A. At first, let your friend know that your friendship is important to you. Also, explain that your relationship needs to stay intact. Secondly, be specific about what is bothering you.

Q. How do you deal with significant others who are being difficult?
A. Reassure your significant other that he or she has many qualities that you respect and enjoy. Secondly, be specific about the issues by agreeing to be open and honest with each other.

Q. Why does shyness cause people to be difficult?
A. Shyness can cause a person to be insecure or overly need the approval of other people. This sets up the appearance of being difficult. Here are five points to use in dealing with a shy person:

1. Try talking in a nonthreatening, lower tone of voice.

2. Create extra personal space between you and that person.
3. Give a shy person enough time to talk.
4. Use nonthreatening body language.
5. Make that person feel accepted and in control.

Q. How do I deal with a person who talks nonstop?
A. Pause and indicate to the person that you want to change the topic.

> "In life, the only security we may have is within ourselves."
>
> **Kenneth R. Petrucci, MSW**

Q. How do you deal with a child when he or she is being difficult?
A. Children have a tendency to not reveal what is bothering them. The first effort should be to discover why the child is acting difficult. Ask your child two direct, simple questions: "Can I ask you a question?" Asking the child this question allows the child to feel in control of the situation which gives him or her more of a desire to cooperate. The second question is "What is bothering you?" Pause and wait for the child's reply.

Q. How can we deal with a person who is difficult because of mental health issues?

A. Point one is to remember that a person experiencing mental health issues at times may not always be in control of his or her actions. Point two is unfortunately at times you may need to set limits with people experiencing mental health issues or present your comments knowing their limitations.

Q. How do you deal with someone who is stubborn?
A. Some people don't realize that they are being stubborn; be brief, decisive and assertive.

Q. How do you deal with someone who is argumentative?
A. Set limits with argumentative people. They lack the ability to set limits on themselves. For example, you may wish to inform them of what you will or will not do.

"Sometimes we have no choice but to set boundaries with people."
Kenneth R. Petrucci, MSW

Q. How do you deal with a person who is a gossiping type?
A. Try to identify the topics a person is gossiping about and attempt to avoid them.

Q. How do you deal with a person who becomes difficult at work?

A. Look for patterns in people when they become difficult. Learn to identify the topics or environments that promote a person's difficult behavior. Attempt to avoid these issues or confront the individual using the phrases in this book from the section entitled "220 Prepared Phrases to Use When Responding to a Person Who Is Being Difficult." Refer to the section in this book titled "How to Deal with Co-Workers When They Become Difficult."

Q. What is the first step in preparing to deal with a difficult situation?

A. Gather as many facts about the situation as you can before you attempt to solve it. Remember not to procrastinate and to take action in an appropriate time frame.

> "Sometimes to be successful we need to take more action. There is no substitute for action."
>
> **Kenneth R. Petrucci, MSW**

WHEN SOMEONE'S BEHAVIOR TOWARDS YOU WILL NOT CHANGE.....

Sometimes we must realize that we may not be able to change another person's negative behavior toward us. If someone is not willing to modify their behavior it is now our responsibility to alter our reactions to that person.

We may need to formulate a new strategy that works for us in dealing with the person who has become difficult.

Do you have a person in your life that you need to take responsibility to formulate a new strategy in dealing with them?

Name of Person:_____

New Strategy:_____

_____

_____

_____

_____

_____

_____

_____

_____

_____

_____

_____

_____

The "Sleep Consciousness State" is ONE OF THE gateways to the use of a greater potential of our minds...

My theory is that there is a state of mind which I refer to as "sleep consciousness." Just prior to falling asleep we can give our subconscious minds a command similar to our search when using a computer to retrieve information from the vast database. When using this technique we are limitless in our inquiries. You can ask any question of your subconscious mind, and then let it go like a balloon rising to the sky. Some of the following examples of questions may be "I would like to know the cure for cancer." "How can I improve my ability to be more successful?" "I would like to know how to improve my financial situation." Your subconscious mind may search for these answers during your sleep consciousness state. It is important that during the day we become receptive to any information that may be given to us as a result of our subconscious mind nighttime search. Remember that when we fall asleep our conscious mind is sleeping and our subconscious mind is awakening. In addition, our dreams may have messages that may help to answer our requested questions. Remember, answers from our subconscious may not be given to us at the time that we expect it. The answers may have their own time frame.

Do you continually try to expand your mental capabilities to be the most you can be?

Yes_____ No _____ Somewhat _____

My new goals to expand my mental capabilities are:

> *"We will never know how far we can go until we reach beyond our highest expectations."*
>
> **Kenneth R. Petrucci, MSW**

INDEPENDENT SELF-STUDY AND SELF-DISCOVERY

Insert the lines you checked off or highlighted in this book that you want to work on or reflect upon, including the quotes in the book.

1. _____ p_____

_____

_____

_____

_____

2. _____ p_____

_____

_____

_____

_____

3. _____ p_____

_____

_____

4. _____ p_____

5. _____ p_____

6. _____ p_____

7. _____ p_____

8. _____ p_____

_____

_____

_____

_____

9. _____ p_____

_____

_____

_____

_____

10. _____ p_____

_____

_____

_____

_____

11. _____ p_____

_____

_____

_____

_____

12. _____ p_____

_____

_____

_____

_____

13. _____ p _____

_____

_____

_____

_____

14. _____ p _____

_____

_____

_____

_____

15. _____ p _____

_____

_____

_____

_____

16. _____ p _____

_____

_____

_____

_____

17._____p_____

_____

_____

_____

_____

18._____p_____

_____

_____

_____

_____

19._____p_____

_____

_____

_____

_____

20._____p_____

_____

_____

_____

_____

21._____p_____

_____

_____

_____

_____

22._____p_____

_____

_____

_____

_____

23._____p_____

_____

_____

_____

_____

24._____p_____

_____

_____

_____

_____

25._____p_____

_____

_____

_____

_____

26. _____ p_____
_____
_____
_____
_____

27. _____ p_____
_____
_____
_____
_____

28. _____ p_____
_____
_____
_____
_____

29. _____ p_____
_____
_____
_____
_____

30. _____ p_____
_____
_____

_____

_____

THE QUALITIES I LIKE ABOUT MYSELF ARE:

_____

_____

_____

_____

_____

_____

THE QUALITIES I WOULD LIKE TO IMPROVE IN MYSELF ARE:

_____

_____

_____

_____

_____

_____

_____

_____

_____

_____

_____

_____

WHAT I LEARNED ABOUT MYSELF FROM READING
THIS BOOK:

_____

_____

_____

_____

_____

_____

_____

_____

_____

_____

_____

> *"We can modify our behavior; don't give up!"*
>
> **Kenneth R. Petrucci, MSW**

> *"It is our responsibility to stop people from taking advantage of our good nature."*
>
> **Kenneth R. Petrucci, MSW**

My immediate goals in dealing effectively with difficult behavior:

> *"It is the advertiser's job to shape our interest. But it is our job to establish our own opinions about what we will and will not purchase...we need to think for ourselves."*
>
> **Kenneth R. Petrucci, MSW**

My short-term goals in dealing with difficult behavior:

> *"Sometimes the fastest way to the front door is through the back door."*
>
> **Kenneth R. Petrucci, MSW**

My long-term goals in dealing with difficult behavior:

> *"If we are closed to constructive criticism, we are closed to self-improvement."*
>
> **Kenneth R. Petrucci, MSW**

> *"Treat yourself as well as your own best friend."*
>
> **Kenneth R. Petrucci, MSW**

Before we organize, eliminate as many distractions as possible. Remember, if we attempt to accomplish more than we can manage, we may find it difficult to be organized. When appropriate, designate a place to work in and arrange like items before we start to organize. Coloring like items the same color can be useful in certain projects, or you can designate certain colors to identify categories.

Five Skills to Organize Your Life

1. Do you create priorities in your life?
   Yes_____ No_____ Somewhat_____
   Setting priorities helps us to identify what is currently most important in our lives.

2. Do you establish systems to work within?
   Yes_____ No_____ Somewhat_____
   Establishing a system or a routine allows us to follow a predictable plan of action thus making us more organized.

3. Do you give yourself enough time to periodically throw away what you don't need?
   Yes_____ No_____ Somewhat_____

It's difficult to remain organized when you develop clutter in your life.

4. Do you assign a place for your items in your life?
    Yes_____ No_____ Somewhat_____
    Consciously assigning a place for your items allows you to remember where you placed them.

5. Do you return items to their assigned places?
    Yes_____ No_____ Somewhat_____
    Returning items to their assigned places stops you from losing them.

> *"Sometimes we never solve a problem because we never identify the real cause."*
>
> **Kenneth R. Petrucci, MSW**

I CAN'T SLEEP, NOW WHAT DO I DO.........?

<u>**The Notebook or Box Method**</u> – place a notebook and a pen or pencil on a surface near your bed and write the word

"Tomorrow" on the notebook. Make a note of whatever is on your mind and write it in your notebook for tomorrow's review. Also, take a box or something similar and write the word "Tomorrow" on it. Create an opening in the box or use a box with a cover. At night if something is concerning or upsetting you, you have the option to write a note about what may be distressful on notebook paper and put it in the box for you to review tomorrow.

Task Method – At the time that you are struggling with sleeping, the task method is asking you to complete a task that you need to get done rather than continuing to wrestle with sleeplessness. Hopefully, you will feel better because you have completed the task rather than contending with insomnia. By completing a task you are redirecting your mind to something positive rather than the negativity of not being able to sleep.

The Spoken Word Method – Another option is to place a tape recorder by your bedside and record any thoughts that may be on your mind which are keeping you from sleeping. Listen to the recording the next day. This may allow you to train your mind to realize that you are not going to forget what is presently occupying your mind because tomorrow you will have the opportunity to deal with these thoughts.

Remember, it is advisable to discuss with your health care professional any extended periods of sleeplessness.

A true fact is only accurate when it is verified.

A percentage of life is a misunder-standing.

Sometimes to be understood is all we need.

Sometimes a hug is all we need.

The invisible world has the answers to the next evolution.

When we step out of our comfort zone we can then explore the world of possibilities.

Be gentle, you never know what is going on in a person's life.

Remember, calories never lie.

When we die all understanding may become unified.

A QUESTIONNAIRE FOR YOU TO DISCOVER IF YOU HAVE ANY OF THESE TWENTY QUALITIES THAT MAKE PEOPLE DIFFICULT:

1. Do you find yourself always needing to exert excessive control when dealing with people?
   Yes_____ No_____ Somewhat_____
   If control is your issue, working to correct it will make it less difficult for people trying to relate to you.

2. Do you make an effort to listen to people?
   Yes_____ No_____ Somewhat_____
   One of the greatest needs human beings have is the need to be listened to. Life becomes less difficult when we are listening to each other.

3. Can you listen to constructive criticism without getting upset?

Yes_____ No_____ Somewhat_____

Most human beings have some personal, unresolved issues. If we can identify some of our own personal issues, this may enable us to work on resolving them and we can become less difficult when interacting with others.

4. Do you talk about problems but never seem to solve them?

Yes_____ No_____ Somewhat_____

It can become difficult when people are always talking with us about problems that never seem to be resolved.

5. Do you have a tendency to complicate matters?

Yes_____ No_____ Somewhat_____

It would be wise to slow down and take enough time to think about a matter before you overreact which could possibly complicate an issue.

6. Do you have a problem admitting that you are wrong?

Yes_____ No_____ Somewhat_____
If we can admit we are wrong, it is the
first step to taking responsibility
for our actions and improving our
lives.

7. Do you always seem to find faults in
people?
Yes_____ No_____ Somewhat_____
If we are always being critical of
others, they may possibly become
withdrawn, very timid, or verbally
or physically aggressive toward you.

8. Do you have a tendency to dwell on
the negative aspects of life?
Yes_____ No_____ Somewhat_____
If we have issues that make us dwell
negatively on things, it is necessary
to identify what is creating the
problems. Develop a strategy to
resolve or cope with the issues.
In general, people know life can
become depressing; therefore they
want to seek a more positive outlook
to offset the negativity in their
lives. Hopefully, we have developed
sound friendships that allow us to

discuss any negative issues in our lives. Seek appropriate counseling when necessary.

9. Do you seem to take things personally?
Yes_____ No_____ Somewhat_____
Most human beings have personal issues that may upset them. However, if we allow our personal issues to create difficulties with others, it may be time to identify our own negative personal issues and work to correct them. Remember to seek counseling when necessary.

10. Do you seem to place yourself above other people?
Yes_____ No_____ Somewhat_____
If someone is always indicating that his or her worth is far greater than the average human being, this may make others feel uncomfortable.

11. Do you frequently argue with people?
Yes_____ No_____ Somewhat_____
Some people feel that arguing on a consistent basis disturbs their

desire to live a healthy and happier lifestyle.

12. Do you often get angry with people?
Yes_____ No_____ Somewhat_____
Some people begin to feel unsafe if someone is constantly getting angry with them.

13. Do you have a strong tendency to want people to live up to your expectations?
Yes_____ No_____ Somewhat_____
Life can become difficult when we are constantly being expected to live up to the expectations of another person.

14. Are you impatient with people on a frequent basis?
Yes_____ No_____ Somewhat_____
Sometimes your impatience with people makes it difficult for them because this can cause them to become stressed and less productive.

15. Do you have a tendency to blame others for your shortcomings on a frequent basis?

Yes_____ No_____ Somewhat_____
If we have a tendency to blame others for our shortcomings, it makes it difficult for people to deal with us and may feel it is an unfair relationship.

16. Do you have a tendency to tell people it's "my way or the highway"?
Yes_____ No_____ Somewhat_____
Some people want to feel that the person they're dealing with is flexible enough to consider all options.

17. Do you take responsibility for your actions?
Yes_____ No_____ Somewhat_____
Not taking responsibility for your actions makes it difficult for you to grow and become a more responsible person.

18. Do you have a tendency to get out of control because of your own obsessive perfectionism when dealing with people?
Yes_____ No_____ Somewhat_____
Striving to be our best is good. However, getting out of control

because we want others to be perfect can make people find us difficult.

19. Do you make it difficult for people who are trying to help you?
Yes_____ No_____ Somewhat_____
If you make it difficult for people to help you they may discontinue trying to assist you.

20. Do you have a tendency to degrade someone you are in conflict with?
Yes_____ No_____ Somewhat_____
Sometimes we degrade other people to lift our low self-esteem.

Commentary about Twenty Major Qualities that can Make People Difficult:

As a psychotherapist and a human being, I realize that we are not perfect; therefore, even if you realize that you have some of these negative issues that could make you difficult, you most certainly have positive traits that make people enjoy you. It is easy to focus on the negatives of our personalities and not acknowledge the positives. We all have pluses and minuses in our personality traits. **Remember to also acknowledge all of your positive traits and set sailing into the world** of self-development and self-improvement. From answering these questions you may become aware of any areas that you can improve upon.

> *"Say goodbye to negative thoughts, and say hello to better health."*
>
> **Kenneth R. Petrucci, MSW**

STOP, THINK, MAKE GOOD CHOICES.

General Notes:

Kenneth R. Petrucci, MSW

"*If we periodically record insights about ourselves into a journal, it will help us to discover who we are.*"

Kenneth R. Petrucci, MSW

"*Some people want you to achieve only to their limitations.*"

Kenneth R. Petrucci, MSW

THE KENNETH R. PETRUCCI, MSW SELF-HELP INFORMATION PROCESS

This self-help information process may help people discover the root causes of many of their problems including weight gain, anxiety, financial problems, gambling, smoking, compulsive shopping, and alcohol or substance abuse, etc.

Carry a small notebook, copy the following questions and record your answers for your review.

<u>Clearly state your problem below:</u>

_____

_____

_____

_____

_____

_____

_____

_____

_____

_____

_____

_____

_____

_____

<u>(Gathering Information Session I)</u>

When you feel your problem is beginning to surface, try to answer these questions; in doing so it is best to pause, take a deep breath, be patient and wait for your answers.

What am I thinking?

_____

_____

_____

_____

What am I feeling?

_____

_____

_____

_____

What am I doing?

_____

_____

_____

_____

What do I need right now?

_____

_____

_____

_____

What environment am I in?

_____

_____

_____

_____

What steps can I take to help myself deal with this problem?

_____

_____

_____

_____

_____

_____

_____

_____

_____

_____

> *"Sometimes what we are not aware of we can become a victim of."*
>
> **Kenneth R. Petrucci, MSW**

Most **compulsive** behaviors have something that **triggers** them. You may use the **Real Cause Method**. Your **answers** in the Self-help Information Process may help you or your counselor to better understand your problem, which also may aid the process of finding a better way to deal with it. This information may also help you to **identify** what triggers your problem. In most compulsive behaviors we get a fulfillment of some kind. An example would be if your answer in the "What am I Thinking Section" was "I would like to smoke to complement my meal." Then you can eat in an environment that does not permit smoking.

In addition, another approach would be to use the **Positive Replacement Method** at the time the compulsive behavior is beginning to surface. A previously prepared replacement could be having a friend available to answer your call should you be thinking about abusing alcohol. Your friend may divert your thinking from alcohol to a friendly discussion. Use your **imagination** to discover some of the prepared replacements you will be able to use.

The last approach would be to identify any **patterns of behavior** that could be triggering your problem. An example would be your response to the question "What Am I Thinking?" in the Self-Help Information Process. Perhaps you discovered after several sessions of gathering information that there is something specifically bothering you that was **repeated**. In order to identify the **compulsive repeated pattern**, you would want to make an attempt to answer the above question a **second** time.

> *"Sometimes it appears that people are having difficulties with us, but the difficulty may be with them."*
>
> **Kenneth R. Petrucci, MSW**

When you feel your problem is beginning to surface again, try to answer these questions:

At this session we are repeating the questions several times in order to reveal if there are any patterns to your behavior problems.

What am I thinking?

_____

_____

_____

_____

What am I feeling?

_____

_____

_____

_____

What am I doing?

_____

_____

_____

_____

What do I need right now?

_____

_____

_____

_____

What time is it?

_____

_____

_____

_____

What environment am I in?

_____

_____

_____

_____

Did you identify any patterns of behavior that could be the cause of the problem?

1.

2.

3.

What steps can I take to help myself deal with this problem?

1.

2.

3.

> "*Opportunities are only as visible as our ability to recognize them.*"
>
> **Kenneth R. Petrucci, MSW**

Do you have an opportunity right now that you can act on?

KEN, I do recognize an opportunity—here it is:

_____

_____

_____

_____

_____

_____

_____

_____

_____

_____

_____

_____

_____

_____

A Journal for Monitoring My Success in Solving My Problems

1.The problem is:

_____

_____

_____

_____

2.My strategies to solve this problem are:

_____

_____

_____

_____

3.What happened after I applied my strategies to solve this problem?

_____

_____

_____

_____

4.What did not work for me using these strategies to solve my problem?

_____

_____

_____

_____

5.What did work for me using these strategies to solve my problem?

_____

_____

_____

_____

6.What can I do to prevent this problem from happening again?

_____

_____

_____

_____

1.The problem is:

_____

_____

_____

_____

2.My strategies to solve this problem are:

_____

_____

_____

_____

3.What happened after I <u>applied</u> my strategies to solve this problem?

_____

_____

_____

_____

4.What did not work for me using these strategies to solve my problem?

_____

_____

_____

_____

5.What did work for me using these strategies to solve my problem?

_____

_____

_____

_____

6.What can I do to prevent this problem from happening again?

_____

_____

_____

_____

1.The problem is:

_____

_____

_____

_____

2.My strategies to solve this problem are:

_____

_____

_____

_____

3.What happened after I <u>applied</u> my strategies to solve this problem?

_____

_____

_____

_____

4.What did not work for me using these strategies to solve my problem?

_____

_____

_____

_____

5.What did work for me using these strategies to solve my problem?

_____

_____

_____

_____

6.What can I do to prevent this problem from happening again?

_____

_____

_____

_____

> *"Sometimes we take responsibility for a problem that is not ours."*
>
> **Kenneth R. Petrucci, MSW**

> *"Sometimes a disappointment may be a blessing in disguise."*
>
> **Kenneth R. Petrucci, MSW**

General Notes

WHAT DO I NEED
TO DO TO ADVANCE MYSELF IN LIFE......?

Take enough time to decide what <u>your true goals are</u>. Develop a plan to achieve them. Perhaps guidance or career counseling will be helpful. If you are unsure whether or not you want to pursue a particular profession try to arrange to volunteer or establish an internship in your career choice. After observing and being involved in your volunteer or internship position it may become evident whether you are correct in pursuing this type of employment.

This may eliminate incurring unnecessary educational debt. A reference librarian may be able to obtain information regarding how to arrange an internship or volunteering in your field of interest. Also, "shadowing" may be available which involves following someone in his or her daily employment activities for a short period of time.

We want to excel in our educational grades to be the best that we can be. They are part of the sum of the whole. They are not the whole. There are many qualities that become factors in people being successful, such as motivation, determination, personality traits, common sense, organizational and communication skills and relating to people, etc.

> *"The true potential of something is sometimes never realized until it is tested."*
>
> **Kenneth R. Petrucci, MSW**

My new goals are:

1. My new goal for the year (insert year):

_____

_____

_____

_____

2. My manageable steps to accomplish this goal:

_____

_____

_____

_____

1. My new goal for the year (insert year):

_____

_____

_____

_____

175

2. My manageable steps to accomplish this goal:

_____

_____

_____

_____

1. My new goal for the year (insert year):

_____

_____

_____

_____

2. My manageable steps to accomplish this goal:

_____

_____

_____

_____

> *"Appreciative living is learning to be grateful for what we have before it is gone."*
>
> **Kenneth R. Petrucci, MSW**

I am grateful for:

1._____

_____

_____

2._____

_____

_____

3._____

_____

_____

4._____

_____

_____

5._____

_____

_____

6._____

_____

_____

7._____

_____

_____

> *"Just being yourself makes you unique."*
>
> **Kenneth R. Petrucci, MSW**

Celebrity quotations and interviews in this book are registered in the Copyright Office in the United States Library of Congress.

Directions for verifying a quotation or audio or visual material in the Copyright Office in the United States Library of Congress are as follows:
www.copyright.gov/records
Click on *Search the Catalog Link*
Enter into *Search for* box
Subject's name "Last Name, First Name"
Example: Petrucci, Kenneth
Click on the name in the *Search By* box
Click *Begin Search*

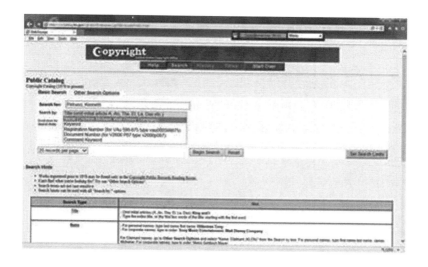

TITLE: *The Man Muhammad Ali Wanted to Be as Great As*
YEAR FILMED: 1976

Muhammad Ali's quotation on the front cover of this book was made during a filmed interview with the legendary World Heavyweight Champion during the filming of his life story, "The Greatest" in 1976. This filmed quote is registered in the Copyright Office in the United States Library of Congress.

Library of Congress Registration Number
PAu003146843
Registration Date: 2007

TITLE: Ernest Borgnine States that Kenneth Petrucci's Writings are "Certainly Outstanding"
YEAR FILMED: 1976

Ernest Borgnine's quotation on the back cover of this book was made during a filmed interview with the legendary actor, star of the classic sitcom McHale's Navy, and Academy Award-winner, on the set while acting in the film, "The Greatest", Muhammad Ali's life story in 1976. This filmed quote is registered in the Copyright Office in the United States Library of Congress.

Library of Congress Registration Number Pau003693844
Registration Date: 2013

TITLE: Ray Charles Interview by Kenneth Petrucci
YEAR RECORDED: 1977
Audio
Library of Congress Registration Number
SRu000672108
Registration Date: 2007

National News Media Coverage of

Kenneth R. Petrucci, MSW

The quotations below regarding Kenneth R. Petrucci, MSW are from major feature articles and are on file at www.wisdom-wagon.com.

YOU ARE NOW BEING TRANSPORTED BACK IN TIME TO THE COOL, LIVELY, TRENDY AND HIP
70's & 80's

"Petrucci with a lusty chuckle unlike the brooding Beethoven..."

Houston Chronicle
By Betty Ewing
2/14/78

"All the good ol' days of radio never saw a host like Petrucci...Petrucci's weekly show, celebrating its third anniversary in May."

Houston Post
By Vicki Nacias, Post Reporter
3/17/80

184

"In his energetic three-hour presentation, Warwick psychotherapist Kenneth R. Petrucci, MSW teaches a course on overcoming procrastination at the Community College of Rhode Island."

Providence Journal

By Ann S. Gooding, Special to the Journal Bulletin

5/10/88

"In truth I lay in comfort or sorrow but I lay knowing"— from <u>Soul's Eye</u> by Kenneth R. Petrucci, MSW

Memphis Press Scimitar

By Ron Harris, Press-Scimitar Staff Writer

12/12/75

Press Women Magazine featured a front-cover, three-page, full-length summary of Mr. Petrucci's negotiation system in 1986 written by Lori Evangelos Kershner. The December 1986 issue of *Press Women Magazine* made the following quote:

"Petrucci...hosted a self-development talk show for four years on KPFT radio in Houston, Texas, where he interviewed stars such as Ray Charles and Joan Rivers."
Press Women Magazine for Media Professionals, was published by the **National Federation of Press Women,** and established since 1937, which still remains today a prestigious organization for professional women in the press.

Kenneth R. Petrucci ..."On behalf of America...reunite as a nation and be <u>the great country we are."</u>

Associated Press, Memphis (AP)
By Doug Stone, Associated Press Writer
5/16/76

"Reading is one of the keys to the world."

Kenneth R. Petrucci, MSW

I dedicate this book to my mother, Philomena Petrucci, and my father, Rocco Petrucci. I inherited my passion for learning from my mother and my gift for writing from my father. My father was a local Rhode Island celebrity and singer and had an operatic voice. He was also known as Smiling Caruso. The following poem was written by my father to my mother while he was dying. My father died when I was seven years old.

To My Dearest Fannie:

**Mourn not my loss, for you have loved me faithfully;
And when the cold dawn breaks through,
Hold up The Cross and pray for me.
Sending you an ocean of love, with a kiss on each wave.**

Love, Caruso

"*To my readers...if you die before me,*
tell my mother, who has passed on,
that I love her and hope to someday
see her again in a spiritual existence."

Kenneth R. Petrucci, MSW

Much Appreciation

I want to thank my academic colleague, the perceptive speech pathologist Bonny Miller, for inspiring me to write this book.

I would also like to express my deep gratitude to my loyal and supportive friends—Dan, an insightful songwriter and member of the unique-sounding band **LUNA-C**, and to the humble sage Jim Quattrucci.

My appreciation to Mary Allcock, of the Busy Bee Bureau, Pawtucket, Rhode Island for her precise typing and secretarial skills; to Katherine Lombardi, Supervisor of Staples in Warwick, Rhode Island for her formatting tips; much praise to Sheila Petrucci, a superb English teacher, for her proofreading and detailed editing; Karen Trouve, President of Paper Chores in Cranston, Rhode Island for her excellent secretarial services, editing and formatting. It was a great benefit to use the services of the city and town reference librarians in Rhode Island.

I would like to extend a standing ovation to my brother, Bobby C. Petrucci for a lifetime of support. He was a concrete foreman for Gilbane Building Company and was respected for his creative solutions to construction problems. He was affectionately referred to as "the doctor". His insights on effective strategies to manage employees were very informative.

It was very meaningful that Sheila and her husband, Richard Petrucci, my cousin, recognized and helped cultivate my writing skills while I was just a teenager.

I have much gratitude for the Mattera family, which is my mother's side of the family, for providing housing for us after my father's early death. The following supportive members of the household were my grandfather Giovanni Giuseppe, a successful self-made business entrepreneur, my loving grandmother Fortuna, both from Italy, and Uncle John, a father figure, Uncle Jerry, my godfather; and Uncle Anthony, who has an innovative, unique, and philosophical side to his personality.

A colossal "thank you" to the innovative Dean Americo Ottaviano for introducing and cultivating the Kenneth Petrucci Seminars at the contemporary Community College of Rhode Island.

AN
ENTERTAINING
PHOTO
JOURNEY
THROUGH
THE AUTHOR'S LIFE

Ken as a
Toddler

"What a cutie—observe those curls !"

Ken on the day of his First Holy Communion

With Godfather Jerry Mattera

Ken as a young stand-up comedian

"Going under the name Kenny Pipe,
Petrucci did an act as a comic for several
seasons in the Cape Cod area....."
            -Associated Press, Memphis (AP)
        By Doug Stone, Associated Press Writer
                            5/2/76

Ken as a young adult

Body Language Exercise
What is Ken's expression saying to you?

_____

_____

_____

_____

_____

_____

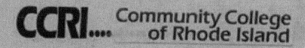

Kenneth Petrucci Seminars

Return to Rhode Island   **10th Successful Year**

Kenneth Petrucci, a popular guest on radio and television, is an author and psycho-therapist from Houston, Texas. He has been recognized for his work in articles by the Associated Press, The Houston Chronicle, Chicago Tribune, Memphis Press Scimitar, and Italian Echo.

"Kenny Petrucci finds reason in life's elusive rhymes."

-Providence Journal, Bert Wade Cole

The dynamic Community College of Rhode Island, known as CCRI, established in 1964, offers various certifications and degree programs.

The Kenneth Petrucci Seminars were presented at CCRI for over ten consecutive years, beginning in 1980.

"In his energetic three-hour presentation, Warwick psychotherapist Kenneth Petrucci...lists ...reasons... why we procrastinate...We feel overwhelmed, we lack information, we seek perfection, we unconsciously dislike a task, or we set unrealistic demands on ourselves."

-Providence Journal
By Ann S. Gooding, Special to the Journal
Bulletin
5/10/88

Ken as a psychotherapist

Ken's Mother and Father

Rocco Petrucci and Philomena (Mattera)
Petrucci, a true spiritual love.

Ken's mother Philomena

"Never let your
heart rule
your mind."
- Philomena
Petrucci

Philomena was born in Italy and came to
America as a child.

(Filly, your hat is wild and your eyes make
our hearts smile.)

ON A SPIRITUAL NOTE ...

During her lifetime, Philomena was a very religious person and known to reach out and help people. Now that she has passed on and is no longer with us, we at Wisdom Wagon, the Publisher of this book, believe in the spiritual world that she will continue this effort to help others. Perhaps she would welcome your thoughts, concerns, or your possible need for guidance.

Ken's Dad, Rocco Petrucci, singing.

"Rocco Petrucci, an opera singer who was known locally as "Smiling Caruso." —The Providence Journal

You can hear Ken's father singing a song by doing a Google search for "Rocco Petrucci Patriotic song" which is on YouTube. This song was written by an outstanding song writer, Joseph Petrucci, my beloved uncle. In the world of opera Rocco's performance of his song was magnificent.

Comments from the <u>1943 Providence Journal</u> newspaper about Rocco Petrucci:

"Petrucci studied for three years at the Boston Conservatory before launching on a career which included the concert stage, light and grand opera. His tenor range reaches F above high C. His most recent public appearance was at Braves Field in Boston where he sang the National Anthem at the opening of a sports program."

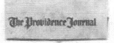

The Providence Journal

Taxidermist Comes To "Caruso's" Rescue

(When Julio Marsella, taxidermist, read the following account of the plight of a local celebrity he was so touched that he offered to use his arts to preserve "Bushy" for the patrons of the Paradise Cafe and for "Smiling Caruso" in particular. His offer was accepted and "Caruso" is somewhat appeased.—Editor)

"Smiling Caruso," the singing bartender at the Paradise Cafe, has lost his smile.

His pet squirrel, Bushy, died suddenly Sunday and the erstwhile smiling Caruso is sad. He'll miss Bushy and so will the boys at the cafe. You see, Bushy and Caruso were partners, they entertained the customers with an act.

Bushy perched on Caruso's shoulder while Caruso slung the beers. He snuggled in his master's pocket, stole nuts from him, scampered around, in and on the cash register while Caruso made change.

"That Bushy!" Caruso said, "he was one, though. Once I thought maybe this wasn't the best place for a little squirrel so I took him in the woods. I even put him up in a tree. But when I went away, he followed me.

"Bushy used to love to hear me sing. When I would hit F above high C he looked at me and seemed to say 'Bravo, bravo.' The other people they didn't know what I was doing. They want to hear the 'Butcher Boy' and that stuff. But Bushy he liked opera."

Rocco Petrucci, Providence Opera singer, will sing for the American Legion at the opening Sundays in the Park program at Roger Williams Park this Sunday afternoon

"SMILING CARUSO" ON PARK PROGRAM

Rocco Petrucci Sings Sunday;

Colonel Waring's Address

Will Be Broadcast.

The photograph on the left makes reference to Rocco's appearance in 1943 on a Sunday at the park program at Roger Williams Park in Providence, Rhode Island

The article on the right was about Rocco's act with his pet squirrel named "Bushy."

"Imagine the daily dialogue between the mind, body and spirit."

Kenneth R. Petrucci, MSW

"Our expectations can unknowingly rule our world."

Kenneth R. Petrucci, MSW

"Meditation sessions remind us that the mind, body and spirit are one."

Kenneth R. Petrucci, MSW

"When we drop our expectations the possibility of disappointments may lessen."

Kenneth R. Petrucci, MSW

Ken as a guest on radio talk shows such as
WPRO, Rhode Island

Ken Hosting his Radio Talk Show, The Creative Connection began in 1977

"Petrucci said his show (is) aimed at self-development of the mind, body and spirit."
Houston Post
By Vicki Macias, Post Reporter
3/17/80

Ken's radio talk show aired for four years on station KPFT 90.1 FM, Houston, Texas. His show raised the consciousness of the general public, which helped make Houston a magical City where your dreams can come true.

Ken as a Radio Talk Show Host

"...Petrucci...garnering comments like these: Mickey Rooney: "In order for anyone to be a success at whatever he is doing in life, he has to accept his individuality. That is the secret key behind everything."

<u>Houston Chronicle</u>
By Betty Ewing, Columnist
2/24/78

"Petrucci says...to be the richest man in the cemetery is only the living dead man's dream." -Associated Press, the Register, Danville, VA May 16, 1976
The above quotation is from _Soul's Eye_ by Kenneth R. Petrucci, MSW.

A profound "thank you" to the libraries at the following universities:
Brown University, University of Memphis, University of Oregon, University of Pittsburgh, Community College of RI -for preserving the first printing of _Soul's Eye_ to be studied, displayed or read by future

generations as it becomes part of the archives of American literature.

Soul's Eye was published by Branden Press, Boston, MA, 1975.

Upon publishing "Richest and Poorest" from *Soul's Eye* by Kenneth R. Petrucci, the Chicago Tribune on June 2, 1974 made the following comment: "Richest and Poorest" uses a cemetery as a symbol of ironic ambitions and doomed materialism." It's been said that Soul's Eye is a passport from this life to the next and that no one should die before reading Soul's Eye by Kenneth R. Petrucci.

On Amazon.com/books Soul's Eye received the highest rating of 5 Stars from a reviewer and its readers.

Customer Review from Amazon.com Books
By Ellie Goldberg, 1/25/14
"Soul's Eye came into my life at a perfect time and spoke to me in a profound way "One day love may come to shore" evoked an image that a fellow sojourner on the path had received for me once about

my destiny being on its way, and I was energized, touched and encouraged by the whole experience.

Review of book from Amazon.com Books
By Samuel Neher, 1/10/11
"Mr. Petrucci is truly a profound writer. If you love the _Prophet_ by Kahil Gibran, then you will love _Soul's Eye_. The book gives many insights into life and teaches you many of life lessons." Readers of the Bible will enjoy the profound spiritual message of Soul's Eye.

TEXAS HISTORY

Which local Texas newspaper published a photo of Kenneth R. Petrucci on the _entire_ front page?

The answer is Suburbia News, Westheimer Edition, Houston, Texas November 19, 1975 Size: 10" x 14".

This photo of Ken, from the back cover of his book _Soul's Eye_, appeared on the front cover of _Suburbia News_.

The mystique of his expression in this photo corresponds to the allure of his writings in _Soul's Eye_.

"Lecturer-radio personality Kenneth R. Petrucci (in) Houston Suburbia newspaper, reviewing his book, splashed the photo over almost the entire front page."

<u>Houston Chronicle</u>
By Betty Ewing, Columnist
2/24/78

Ken as a guest on talk shows

Ken is a guest on WJAR Channel 10 in Rhode Island.

Ken as a guest on Channel 26 Metromedia, Houston, Texas.

"Petrucci...I want to share my triumph and tragedy with people."

-Associated Press

By Doug Stone, Associated Press Writer
Featured in Register, Danville, VA
May 16, 1976

Ken explores a new art form

THE MYSTERIOUS INNER SELF

Ken earned an Associate's Degree in Liberal Arts and a Bachelor of Fine Arts Degree. He has an interest in exploring a new style of art which captures the inner self of a human being. His first attempt in the past was this self portrait (above) of his own inner self. This method of art would be using ones intuition to draw the invisible self of others or oneself. The original drawing is a captivating colorful array of intriguing purple, night-time blue, lipstick red, mustard yellow and vegetable green.

We at Wisdom-Wagon.com, the publishers of this book, upon witnessing the original drawing of Ken's mysterious inner self, stopped delivering wisdom, got off our wisdom wagon, dusted off the wisdom from our shoes, and remained speechless.

This form of art will help an individual to develop their intuition.

A caricature of Ken

In this caricature, the artist is having fun with Ken's personality.

Let the useful wisdom, insights, techniques and practical methods in this book help you to live a more effective and successful life.

www.wisdom-wagon.com

Keep smiling...
Remember smiling helps us to generate our
own happiness.